Words From My Father

David Weber

Published by Waldorf Publishing
2140 Hall Johnson Road
#102-345
Grapevine, Texas 76051
www.WaldorfPublishing.com

Words From My Father

ISBN: 978-1-945177-59-0
Library of Congress Control Number: 2016957019

Copyright © 2017

For my children...

Occasionally there has been reflection on how this started and how it came to be a book. At first there was just the urge to write something to send in a note to family. Each was just a few thoughts that would not be at peace until written and sent.

After some time, it became apparent it was the Holy Spirit planting the seeds for each note, and then helping me write the words as it needed to be told. Still, every note is sent wrapped in the hope and the prayer that I got it right.

When approached about doing a book, it seemed this random collection of notes would not make a viable book. Then, after putting it together, I could see the threads He had created – stories of living our faith. It became apparent this was his plan all along.

Why He picks such unworthy people to do his work is a mystery - it seems this is how Jesus picked his workers all along. In John 1:27, John the Baptist speaks of this, "The strap of whose sandal I am not worthy to untie."

Turns out he has work for all of us, and I rejoice that he has given me this to do for him.

David Weber

Table of Contents

Early Writings

"I tremble for my country when I reflect that God is just; that His justice cannot sleep forever."

— President Thomas Jefferson, 1781

"It is when a people forget God that tyrants forge their chains."

— Patrick Henry, Founding Father

The Center of Moments

Some years ago I heard an interesting radio commentary on a concept he called the "Center of Moments." As he explained, our lives can easily be compared to the journey of a ship at sea. A ship can choose a course and stay with it or make many turns. There will be calm seas with smooth sailing, there will be bright, beautiful days, and there will be storms that cause the boat to pitch wildly up and down.

Standing at the bow or stern of the boat during the storm makes the pitching all the worse. If you are at the center of the boat, the motion is at its' least. This is called the Center of Moments. Our radio commentator went on to encourage us all to find our Center of Moments when we are in a stormy time of life. So much easier to not feel so tossed about and to see the storm for what it is. Good advice and perhaps the commentator left out what he knew we would discover on our own – that God is our Center of Moments.

This Christmas, remember what it is we are celebrating and thank God for all the glorious bright days, for all the smooth sailing and for being our Center of Moments.

Talking about Faith - March 20, 2009

Saturday, Dominic and I attended the funeral of an old friend, Chuck Gage. Chuck was one of the guys in our group that played cards once a month in the Farmington Hills sub. He had had a long bout with emphysema. At the funeral, I had the opportunity to catch up with almost all the guys that played in the card group and their wives who hosted the monthly events.

Looking back, as I was driving home, I realized how many times that afternoon's conversations had turned to a discussion of our faith. Always starting with talk of the kids and easing in and out of conversations of thanksgiving, God's presence in our journey and the peace he has given us. Never had we discussed our faith in all the years we played cards. Maybe it was the funeral setting or our advancing age or just our own maturing in our faith.

During the service, Chuck's son shared a letter with us that he had written to his father three years ago. Prompting the letter had been a fishing trip where Chuck shared with his son his new found faith and the difference it made in his life. The letter, though reminiscent of many things, was rejoicing in his father's spiritual awakening.

Then Sunday, as the mind wanders during Mass, I notice many friends and acquaintances there. Recalling past conversations with these dear people, it is clear how comfortable so many are with their faith and how solid they are in how it fits their lives and the world around us. Knowing what some have been through, I know it is their faith that carried them.

Even the email exchanged with family and friends - there was a time it was mostly jokes. Now faith-filled and inspirational messages fill my inbox. Interesting how much more connected we are with these messages than with the jokes.

Reflecting on this, I then recall a recent media headline about a new poll that showed America was losing its religion. Obviously, they got it wrong. America is coming back to God. Maybe they are starting their journey to their faith later in life, but they are coming.

I hope that I have been, and will continue to be, a helping hand in any journey I can touch.

A Ski Trip to Remember - November 19, 2009

A recent Weber Family tradition is our annual ski trip up north with as many in the family as can make it. Mom and Dad fly up from South Carolina and all the brothers come with their families. Sandy always finds the place to stay – her negotiation skill keeps the cost down for everyone.

We are all staying in the same house and had a rousing good ski on Saturday. What a great family hobby – ski all day, gather at lunch, go to Mass together, dinner together, a little relaxing and everyone is off to bed exhausted. Get up and do it again on Sunday. What a great time.

Dominic begins coughing in his sleep around 2:00 AM Sunday morning. After awhile the coughing becomes more persistent, and he is awake but trying to sleep. Ryan is in the room as well, so I take Dominic out to the living room. We sit in the chair and his coughing gets worse, and now his breathing is getting noisy as the allergy induced asthma kicks in. This is such a rare event I had forgotten to bring the Benadryl.

Sandy comes out, woken by the coughing. She offers help, but they don't have any allergy medicine. I go out to start the car to warm it up to take Dominic to the hospital. We sit there waiting for the car to warm and the coughing and breathing get worse. I have started silently praying.

Dominic doesn't cry, he never even whimpers or complains in the slightest.

Without looking at me he asks "Dad, will I die now."

"You will not die now." Is pretty much all I can spit out.

It is the next and following days before I feel any real clarity on what an incredible question that was. He was only five, but he was not afraid. He just wanted to know what was going to happen.

Sandy finds some Nyquil in a medicine cabinet. We do our best to calculate a child's dose and then give it to Dominic. Fifteen minutes later he is sound asleep in my lap, breathing normally with no cough. I lay him down, thank Sandy, go out to turn the car off and then go to sleep thanking God.

Next morning is truly glorious – the sun is shining and everyone is scrambling to get to the ski hill. Ryan McComb steps into my room and closes the door behind him. He hesitates seeing the question mark on my face and then proceeds to ask for Katie's hand in marriage. I want to give him a big hug, but instead shake his hand and say yes that I would be glad to have him as a son-in-law. Truth is I want to run and shout it to everyone how happy I am to have them marry and have him as a son-in-law. Ryan is waiting until Easter in South Carolina to ask Katie, so I also must wait.

Speaking as a parent, every day is a great day - some more memorable than others. My head was spinning from the events of this weekend and never took time to write them down. This morning, the Thursday before Thanksgiving, 2009, Dominic and I are discussing Thanksgiving and how it is a celebration of giving thanks to God for all the good things he brings to our life.

Reflecting on the many things for which I am thankful, the recollection of this weekend comes to mind. Then it proceeds to run over and over again in my head, forcing me to write it down. So this is why you had to take time to read this letter – Thanksgiving is upon us, and I am asked to share something for which I am truly thankful - all of you.

Pauline - February 25, 2010

Dean's family had gathered Saturday afternoon at his mom's house. Mike was in from Vegas with his family and Paula was there with all of hers. Dean had asked me to come and take some pictures. It was the first time meeting some, and I had not seen many in years.

Surrounded by a number of her grandchildren, Pauline was sitting by the window in the corner of her living room. Dominic immediately went off with Julie to play in the basement. Marilyn and I wandered into the kitchen as I clumsily tried to say hello to everyone, remember all the names and try to remember to introduce Marilyn. I did pretty badly at both.

Then I'm walking over to say hello to Pauline feeling apprehensive. I've known her for over 40 years, yet I don't know what to say to this wonderful person who is facing pancreatic cancer. There she is talking joyously with her grandchildren. Pauline takes the conversation lead – intuitively putting everyone at ease.

She tells us where the illness stands – it hasn't grown over the last two visits, she is not going to do chemo and it seems the doctors are speculating there are perhaps six months. Quickly she adds that she is 88 and has had a good life. I'm sure there are none that would argue with that. Her doctor feels the longevity outlook is the same with chemo as without.

There is no sense that she is putting on a brave face – she has faced it and is going to enjoy every day, and she is instinctively helping all the family to do the same. Pauline is just enjoying the day. Perhaps that is it, spending time with the family is about as good as life can be.

After the picture taking, they get out old slides and old family movies. We watch a little but have to get Dominic to his school talent show. He'll be playing Beethoven on the keyboard. On the drive out Marilyn and I talk quietly about our visit.

Tears fill my eyes the next day during Mass as I prayed for Pauline and her family. The world is a better place having had the privilege of Pauline Williams being with us these 88 years. Please join me in praying for her and her family during this time.

Unalienable Rights - April 18, 2010

On occasion, our country's leaders have had important things to say. Founded in truth and carrying importance to our lives and our children's. Mostly these words go unheeded, washed away by the inevitable onslaught of half-truths and sound bites.

Makes you wonder how our country's founders were able to create this nation. How was it that their great words were written and not washed away? Instead there was created the Declaration of Independence and then The Constitution. Incredible documents, creating a great nation. How is it that these men achieved more than anyone could possibly have dreamed?

Some might have guessed the possibilities from the Declaration of Independence – such powerful words have seldom been written:

"We hold these truths to be self-evident, that all men are created equal, that they are endowed by their Creator with certain unalienable rights, that among these are Life, Liberty and the pursuit of Happiness."

It is true, many were great men and many were great leaders. Yet there have been many great men and many great leaders, some making a real difference, but creating

11

this great nation is a thing of wonder. Was it that these men were driven to do the right thing?

Having risked everything and made such sacrifice, was it that they would not walk away until they had created something worthy of that sacrifice. All were in, and they would win together or lose everything together. Was it knowledge of the risk and sacrifice undertaken by all that brought a respect for one another to cause them to listen and recognize when truth was spoken. Or was it their constant prayer and trust in God that brought us here, or, simply God's hand creating a safe place for all.

Today there is debate over the existence of truth, any truth. I believe, as do many of you, that there are simple truths in this world that cannot be denied by honest men. **"Men occasionally stumble over the truth, but most of them pick themselves up and hurry off as if nothing had happened." Sir Winston Churchill.**

There will be great leaders again that come speaking truth, hopefully soon, hopefully this fall. But again the torrent will come to drown their words and the sound of their supporters. Let us not be quieted. While we have breath, let us exercise our freedom of speech. While we can still kneel, let us pray for this country, and, ask God to help us deliver on the first of those unalienable rights – the right to life.

Tears of Thanksgiving - November 25, 2010

In younger days I recall noticing people with tears flowing down their face in the middle of a regular Sunday Mass. It was troubling to see and even more so when it is someone in your own family. It seemed there must be something very sad and difficult going on in their life. Turns out I was probably wrong about that most of the time, if not all.

After years away from the church, it was Katie, Becca, and Ryan that brought me back. As they started Catechism, we started attending church. After awhile, maybe a long while, I'm there because I want to be there. Occasionally the gratitude to God for these three children is overwhelming during Mass and I end up fighting back tears. Never occurs to me that others with joyous and thankful thoughts are perhaps those same people I see with tears flowing.

At the 18-week ultrasound we found out Dominic had a heart defect. Visiting with teams of doctors and then Dr. Ohye at U of M, Dominic's birth plan becomes clear. He will be born at U of M and then at four days old he is to have open heart surgery.

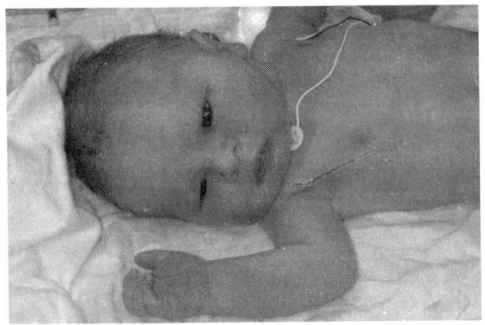

One evening at a St Patrick's social gathering we are relating the heart issues that our unborn baby is facing. A friend went over and took Father Fred's arm and brought him over. A group of us went into the church and Father Fred did the anointing of the sick. Describing what followed is not possible except that we knew then that Dominic would get through it just fine.

Then he is born, and he is as beautiful and vibrant as any child. Four days later he has the surgery. We come back into the ICU and seeing his lifeless body takes every bit of life out of me. His chest rises and falls to the soft click of the ventilator. Tubes are connected to him everywhere. A monitor overhead reads out his life signs. To this day, whenever I think of that moment, tears run down my face as they are at this moment.

Our first Sunday back at church with Dominic, the tears ran down my face much of the Mass. They were tears of gratitude and thanksgiving but also of sorrow. God had told us, plain as day, at the anointing of the sick that

Dominic would be fine. My weak faith lost hold of that on that day in the ICU.

Nowadays I can hardly get through a single Mass without having to wipe tears from my eyes. But these are tears of Thanksgiving. So if you see someone crying during Mass, do not be troubled. There is so much to be thankful for, it frequently overwhelms. There are these four great kids, a great son-in-law, a woman who loves me, a large and wonderful family and great friends. Like I said, sometimes it overwhelms.

God Bless and Happy Thanksgiving.

2011

"Duty is ours; results are God's."
— President John Quincy Adams

"Statesmen, my dear Sir, may plan and speculate for liberty, but it is Religion and Morality alone, which can establish the Principles upon which Freedom can securely stand."
— John Adams, 1776

"Only a virtuous people are capable of freedom. As nations become more corrupt and vicious, they have more need of masters."
— Benjamin Franklin, 1787

Sharing the Load - February 10, 2011

Weekday mornings start with a bowl of cereal and orange juice while reading email, which explains why you only get emails from me before 6:30 in the morning. Carepages emails have been a steady part of the inbox for the last few weeks. Carepages is a website families use to keep everyone updated on the doings and progress of an ill or injured family member. It was a new thing eight and one-half years ago when Dominic was born.

Reading the Carepages emails becomes the first event every morning. As the inbox fills, the mouse finds its way to the Carepages email all by itself. There are reports of the patient's and family's progress and activities. There are some notes posted from well-wishers and some pictures. Not being a member of the family I am reluctant to post a note, but it gets posted anyway letting them know we are praying for them every day.

Notes of prayer, encouragement, and support flow down the pages. Every note of prayer feels like a small victory – one more person praying is one more person giving the greatest gift there is. It is much the same as hearing a name on the prayer list at Mass of someone you care about; a wonderful thought to have so many people praying for them. Stories of the gatherings and doings of the supporters also fill the pages. It must be both overwhelming and humbling to the families and the patient.

Rejoicing in the love and support shown to these families, you marvel at the goodness of so many people. A burden is being shared by all, lightening the load for the patient and family.

Recalling eight and one-half years ago, I marveled then at how many people were praying for Dominic and all of us. It was humbling. Every day it seemed more people told us of more people praying for Dominic. My parents alone seemed to have enlisted half of the country and parts of Europe into prayer service. A burden was shared and the only way to thank all of them is to do it in turn for others at each opportunity.

One line from a beautiful poem reads "I asked God to spare me pain. God said, No. Suffering draws you apart from worldly cares and brings you closer to me." Seems it is true for all involved – the patient, the family and all the friends and supporters. All are taking a pause from their day to bring love and support; Christ's love and support. All are reading or hearing of the notes of prayer. All these people coming together in prayer is perhaps doing a bit more than bringing God's grace to the patient and family – it is bringing to all who read and hear it, as well bringing it to any not inclined to prayer.

Like the saying goes; Love like you've never been hurt, dance like no one is watching... Let's add "Pray like it is the best gift you could ever give." I pray for each of you every day. I invite you to join. Let us invite everyone to join.

Giving up stuff for Lent - March 22, 2011

It was the first Friday of Lent, and Dominic and I are having breakfast and discussing the Ash Wednesday Fish Fry and the next one coming this evening. Dominic looks at me with some intensity as he explains how he had tried to give up candy for Lent in past years but that it was just too hard. As his look turns sheepish, he says he has given up something kind of silly this year. He has given up getting angry with his best friend, Griffin.

Recognizing this as possibly one of the precious teaching moments, I ask does he get angry with Griffin often. Apparently, this is almost a daily cycle – playing together, getting angry at each other, and then resolving their anger.

I tell Dominic that "giving up getting angry at Griffin" is a very grown up thing to do for Lent. It requires forgiveness and controlling your anger, both of which are very grown up things to work on for Lent. Plowing on with my teaching moment, I explain that many things worth doing are too difficult without God's help. Giving up candy or not getting angry with Griffin are both difficult to do. Ask God for help with these. Later you will see what a difference it made.

Dominic agrees that controlling your anger is a tough one, but, "Turns out, when I don't get angry at Griffin, then Griffin doesn't get angry at me."

I'm thinking, Wow, what a different world we would have if every person held onto these lessons learned in elementary school. And once again, the student has become the teacher and the teacher the student.

Serving one Another - April 22, 2011

Sunday morning, our first spring break morning at Mom and Dad's house on Seabrook, Dad heads off to church early because he is the altar server at today's 9:30 Mass. I recall commenting how life had come full circle – being an altar server at eight-years-old and now at 81-years- old.

During Mass, I couldn't help but notice how my father performed his duties as an altar server with all the seriousness and genuineness of an eight-year-old intent on doing every part correctly. Something worth pondering when you also know that this is the same man that played key roles building small companies into large corporations.

Tuesday is rainy so we head into Charleston to visit some favorite spots. Mom and Dad both volunteer at Habitat for Humanity's resale shop which is a major source of Habitat's funds to build homes for families in need. I had asked Mom if we could stop in to see the shop on the way back from Charleston, having heard so much about it over the years. We had a large group spread between two cars. Mom was riding with me and Dad had the grandkids.

Two ladies were at the checkout counter as we came in the door - their faces lit up like some celebrity had just walked through the door. Mom introduces us - Greg and Wendy, Marilyn and me. The two ladies at the counter are quick to tell us "We like Betty." For a moment I wonder at this reception that Mom has received. Perhaps they are just proud that Mom brought in some family to show off the place.

Awhile later Dad walks in with the grandkids and they are just as excited to see Dad. As Mom showed us around and we had the chance to visit with some of the volunteers, it becomes clear how much they are valued here. My guess is it is as much for their energy and cheerfulness as for the work they do. It may seem a small thing to my parents, this time that they spend at Habitat, given the countless hours they have spent in service to others over the years. But, it is a big thing to the people they are helping and to their fellow volunteers.

Later I think of my friends and fellow volunteers at St. Patrick's that serve our parish and the community. And, there are so many more friends serving quietly, being part of the answer. My brothers and their families, as well, serving God in service to others. It is humbling to have so many good people to count as friends, to have such parents and such a family, and yet, it also feels like a great honor. Perhaps this is part of the reason the Habitat people were gladdened by my parents' visit. Perhaps the same as to why I am always so gladdened to see all of you.

As the mind travels in these thoughts, I am reminded of many different messages; two in particular – the call to live our faith and the words of St. Francis of Assisi, "Evangelize always; sometimes use words." The first, gratefully we are reminded of frequently. The second, someone in our bible study group had brought up at last week's session.

Yesterday's Holy Thursday Mass includes the washing of the feet; Jesus' example to his apostles. Father Tom focuses on this in his homily, how Jesus was teaching us how to serve one another and to have our example teach others.

May God bless you and may you have a glorious Easter.

Keeping your Eye on the Ball - June 27, 2011

In baseball, making contact with the ball is mostly just keeping your eye on the ball - something repeated constantly by coaches and parents to their young prodigies. And something Dominic hears from me every time he gets up to bat, to the point where I get dirty looks from the batter's box if I said it one too many times or too loudly.

He was struggling with his batting early in the season, striking out two out of three times at bat and on occasion not getting a hit. Several games into the season I showed him pictures of himself batting, zoomed in, where he could see that either his eyes were closed or he was looking at the coach and not the ball. His reaction – "I had no idea." Telling him he didn't get it, showing him he understood.

Our whole team was struggling with batting and at the next game coach Rob ran the boys through batting drills for a half hour before the game. Batting was dramatically better for every boy that game with the team scoring over 20 runs. Dominic had two solid hits out of three times at bat.

Batting drills were conducted for every game after that resulting in a lot of scoring and a lot of wins. Dominic continued getting two and three hits out of three times at bat every game. Still, every time at bat, he heard the mantra from me of keeping your eye on the ball. If he struck out, he would quickly get to the bench to avoid any additional pointers from me.

Late in the season I missed one of his games being in Columbus for a cousin's wedding. The game was at 10:00 AM on a Saturday – the same time we are on the road to Columbus. Marilyn, my brother Steve and his wife Sandy are in the car with me. Patti calls after Dominic's first at bat. He had struck out and had gone to Patti with tears in his eyes saying, "I need my dad; I need my dad here to yell at me." It was all I could do just to keep the tears from flowing down my face.

Perception is an interesting thing – what is coaching to us is "being yelled at" to them. I'll have to work on that. Interesting though how kids know that they need and want the coaching – need and want the parenting, regardless of how much they resist.

Seems it is true for us as well; we all need and want God in our everyday life; regardless of how much we resist.

Celebrating Success - July 8, 2011

Baseball season with a bunch of eight-year-old boys is a real hoot. They have been playing for a few years now but staying focused on the game is still a struggle for many of them. Their hitting, catching and throwing skills improve each year and visibly during the season. Aside from the boys having a lot of fun, we hope they learn sportsmanship and develop a love of sports.

Dominic is enjoying baseball, but being the smallest on the team (always), he is not one of the better players. Some of the better players do get frustrated sometimes when teammates don't make the catch or make a bad throw. It's a natural reaction because they want to win. Winning is important to them but not quite as much as getting a hit and making the play when the ball comes to them - seems true for the parents as well.

Then there is the end of the game ritual after congratulating the other team on a good game. The team retires to second base for the coach's pep talk and all-

important presentation of the game ball. A game ball is something akin to an Academy Award to these boys. You can see the anticipation on their faces, each boy hoping beyond hope it is his this time. Perhaps recounting some of the game events to themselves, justifying in their mind why they might be worthy to receive it, or not.

Our first Wednesday night game was a big event for Dominic. The third inning he was playing the Pitcher position – a machine does the actual pitching. The batter hits a grounder towards him; he runs, scoops it up and throws it to the first baseman to get the out. Something that happens in baseball many times every game, but this was Dominic's first, ever.

He came close to making two more throws for outs that inning. Fifth inning he is playing second base. Another grounder to him and he makes the throw to the first baseman for another out. There is joy in Mudville tonight.

After the game, the boys are gathered around the coaches at the second base gathering spot. The boys are

pumped from winning their second game in a row after a big loss in game one. Dominic is awarded the game ball for his two defensive plays and a nice hit down the third baseline.

Quickly each of the boys congratulates him in a flurry of high-fives, fist pounds, and other such things. There are no sour faces, no sulking, just celebrating with Dominic his moment. They could have groused about Dominic's missed plays or their own stellar plays or hits that should have gotten them the game ball. But they didn't. These are good boys and my admiration for them grew as I watched and reflected on that simple act.

Later, trying to gauge Dominic's impression, I was asking him, "What was that chicken wing thing you guys were doing?" Dominic explains with a laugh, "Dad, that's a man hug." Who knew?

This gift to celebrate someone else's success seems to require a level of graciousness that has not always been there for me. Then to see this in a bunch of eight-year-old boys… I'm thinking that I was a typical selfish eight-year-old nearly fifty years ago.

Near the end of the season we are playing the first-place team again. We are losing by a lot, and the boys are more into this game than any other. They are cheering each other and celebrating every hit and every play like it was tied up in the ninth inning of the World Series. How is it that these boys have these shining moments? Perhaps it is simply the coaching; coaching the kids to properly congratulate the other team after the game, to cheer their teammates on.

As the season goes on, I can see it in the coaching. Valuable coaching moments include congratulating players on a good play, including those on the other team. Game ball presentations come with reminders that several could have gotten the game ball that game and demonstrating that all team members are valued by finding a reason to get at least one game ball to each of the boys over the season; and on.

Seems this ability to love one another, as commanded by our maker, can be learned and shared in many ways. Celebrating someone else's success is one. Like the sign says "Sportsmanship – Pass it on."

Magic Glasses - August 11, 2011

Imagine that God gave us magic glasses with which to view the majesty of his creation.

What if those magic glasses could reveal the warmth of God's love for us.

What if those magic glasses could reveal God's grace being shed upon us?

What if those magic glasses could show us how precious each of our lives is to God.

What do you think we might see through those magic glasses?

What if all this were true and we did not know it was from God.

Then truly we have eyes and do not see.

Guardian Angels - September 10, 2011

Dominic and I are finishing breakfast the morning after his ninth birthday and whooping it up about our swim fest at the sandbar the previous night. Kelly House, with kids Jake and Samantha and Jake's friend Ben, had stopped by on their pontoon and had taken us all out to the sandbar. Other kids arrived, and there were maybe ten kids playing on the white foam rafts.

King of the Hill is a favorite game on these rafts. It's a rough and tumble game the kids love. Dominic had seemed unfazed at being the smallest. Occasional strategic alliances helped him stay on the raft longer. This is his first summer swimming in the deep water without a life jacket. So I had watched with pride and no small amount of trepidation as he swam some distances between rafts, back to the shallows, and from the shallow to the raft again.

Dominic is commenting on the amount of time spent in the deep water last night. Asking if he was scared he says, "No, I knew that God was with me." Great answer, but concern that he may get over confident causes me to point out that, "It is still you that has to swim. God and your guardian angel are there to help keep you from harm, but you still have to do the swimming."

Reminded by the mention of guardian angels, something we had touched on in Tuesday's Bible study, I

36

tell Dominic I have something to show him, and I go and get my Bible. Matthew 18:10, Jesus is telling the disciples that unless they become like children, they shall not enter the Kingdom of Heaven. Jesus went on to tell of the woe that shall come to anyone that would lead a child to sin, and this is where he tells us of the children's guardian angels.

Hugging me Dominic answers, "I feel like you are my guardian angel sometimes. You warm me up when I'm cold, you keep me safe…"

"Feeling warm from the inside out I tell him, "Yes, God does give you a mom and a dad to watch over you, guide you, keep you warm…."

Some weeks prior, Dominic had asked me if I believed in guardian angels. "I certainly do," I had answered. He asked if I had ever seen mine. "I think I may have seen glimpses – just a motion in my peripheral vision that is gone when I look to see what it was" was my answer. What I don't elaborate on is that this happens in times of trouble when I am hanging on to God with both hands. No way to know whether this is my guardian angel there protecting me or Satan waiting for me to lose my trust in God, or, just old eyes playing tricks. Regardless, I will continue to hang on to God with both hands and trust him, always.

Pulling me back from these thoughts was Dominic saying that he had seen his guardian angel once. I don't know what to make of this so I ask him a bit about it and he asks if I believe him. "Yes, I do believe you," I answer. Truth is I do believe him and yet I don't know what to make of it.

That seems to happen a lot these days – things happen, and questions arise that are beyond my knowing or understanding. Nothing to do with it except give thanks to God and to trust in him, always. Seems God only expects us to trust him, give him our best every day and we are allowed to leave the rest to him – we'll get the answers in Heaven.

Scouting for Food - November 19, 2011

Last Saturday was our annual Scouting for Food collection day. It's a council-wide event that last year gathered 392,000 pounds of food for Gleaners Food Bank, helping to feed so many in need.

Last year was our den's first time doing the food drive. One of the other leaders had brought the bags to a parent/leader meeting to see if any of the dens were interested in helping. Having served on the council board for the past many years, I knew what an important event this was, so I signed us up.

Our strategy is to tie the bags to the door of every home and then return the following Saturday to collect the food. Imprinted on the bags are instructions asking for the filled bag to be left on the porch by 9 AM on the designated date.

Perhaps the first thing that strikes you is how many boys and parents are willing to spend several hours on two different Saturdays, distributing the bags and then collecting the filled bags. Next, you notice that almost every person that sees the boys distributing the bags, asks what the boys are working on – they recognize the uniform the boys are wearing. Then they want to fill a bag for you right then.

Collection day you would think the boys are on a treasure hunt. Every bag on a porch is another victory, racing each other to retrieve the lost treasure. Both days are exhausting for the boys as they run from house to house and back to the cars. But collection day their exhaustion is triumphant as they admire the pile of bags in the back of the vans and SUVs.

Reflecting on these thoughts, I'm filled with pride for our neighbors who donate so much food without needing a receipt or even a thank you. I'm filled with pride for our boys and our parents that all chip in so happily to do this. I'm filled with pride for our Boy Scout Council that commits so much of its scarce resources to create this incredible event of caring for one another.

How does it come to be that so many serve their task to make this happen? Is it that we are all just caring for each other as God commanded us? Yes, but it also seems it is because someone asked. Our Council asked the Boy Scout and Cub Scout leaders, the Troup and Pack leaders asked the parents and boys, and the boys asked the neighbors with a bag imprinted with instructions.

Perhaps you see the picture as I do – God works through us, each of us. When someone asks for help in caring for others, many respond. Perhaps it is the reminder of what God has asked of us, or it is just there, imprinted on your hearts. When you ask, many will respond. Who am I to ask, I wonder. The same as you, one asked by God to serve one another.

As our Thanksgiving holiday approaches, I am thankful that we have filled the Gleaners food bank to brighten the day for so many. I am thankful for all of those that were part of it. I am thankful for all of you, my family and friends. I am thankful and amazed at the blessings God has given all of us.

May you and yours have a blessed Thanksgiving.

Canyons - December 30, 2011

Monday, December 19, 2011, we are at the Canyons ski resort in Utah. It is day four of the Weber family Utah trip and all 12 from this year's group are skiing Echo, a challenging blue. It's a bit icy, and we are on the last steep face before we get back on the Sun Peak chair. No new snow with big crowds seems to always create icy conditions by afternoon.

Dominic follows me on the blue runs, staying close behind and following my path. I'm always doing the rubber neck thing, looking back to check on him and looking forward to the hill ahead.

Looking back at Dominic, I see a woman come over the rise at high speed in a slight crouch, skiing the right side of the hill. Continuing onto the steep face, never making a turn, she was accelerating. We're also skiing the

right side of the hill are Mom, 81, and Dad, 82, ahead of us.
I turn and head to the center of the hill, drawing Dominic
with me; the process to avoid reckless skiers such as this
one. She flies past bumping into a guy in a brown ski suit.

Turning to look downhill, just as I catch sight of the
girl again, she smashes into my mother. In the cloud of
snow and flying equipment, Mom is not moving. She is as
limp as a rag doll and making no move to stop herself as
she tumbles down the hill. We are headed to Mom and can
hear Dad yelling, "Oh no, oh no," over and over again as he
skis down to her. I'm already praying.

Mom is lying still face down in the snow, head pointed
downhill. One arm is above her head, and the other beside
her. There is a little blood coming from her nose. Putting
my face next to hers, I can hear her breathing and some of
the knot leaves my throat. She is actually softly snoring –
somehow this also helps to loosen the knot in my stomach.

Some guy skis up and calls 911, apparently somehow
knowing the process to get the 911 operator to patch him
through to the Canyons ski patrol and then skillfully
explains the situation. A ski patrol arrives within a couple
of minutes as Mom is starting to come to.

The ski patrol wants Mom to stay still, face down in
the snow, head downhill, until he can get her neck
supported. Mom wants to get up and the ski patrol is trying

to make her lie still. I know my mom and I know the outcome of this struggle. Mom gets up. Quickly the ski patrol goes to support her neck as she sits up. He is asking if any of us are trained for support of neck injuries. My brother Jeff knows that his wife Marilyn is EMS-trained and calls for her.

He has Marilyn support her neck as he begins his process. He asks us and Mom a bunch of questions, all the time radioing in his information. Mom clearly has concussion symptoms, but she tells the ski patrol, "I think I can ski down on my own." I think we would have all laughed out loud had we not been so scared. Another ski patrol arrives and they begin the process of getting Mom onto a backboard and into the sled. All the while Mom keeps apologizing to everyone for messing up their ski vacation. No amount of explaining will dissuade her that this is none of her fault. We tell her what happened, but it doesn't seem to make sense to her because she can't remember it.

Jeff had put crossed skis in the snow above our group - the universal skiing distress signal. Despite the marker, a careless snowboarder crashes into the crossed skis. The ski patrol threatens to pull his season pass and yet the snowboarder wants to argue. I'm guessing my brothers and I would have rearranged the guys' attitude had we not been so focused on Mom. Jessie, Chase, and Jason take up traffic cop roles to prevent further incident.

My brothers and I are enlisted to help get her turned on her side, onto the backboard, and then into the sled. Everyone is moving carefully to avoid any slips on the icy steep slope. They have put Mom in a neck brace and foam blocks to hold her head still. Mom is very uncomfortable from the neck brace and complains someone is pressing on her leg. Several times Mom mentioned someone pressing on her leg, but no one was.

They take Mom down in the sled and the 11 of us follow. There is a point in the trail down where you catch a tow rope up to continue the trail down. There is a snowmobile waiting as the sled arrives at the tow rope. In one fluid motion, the sled is connected to the snowmobile, and it pulls the sled the rest of the way to the first aid station. At the station, Mom and backboard are transferred to a stretcher and quickly taken into an exam room.

Canyons' first aid station is staffed by well-trained nurses and a doctor, Dr. Wynn, who was seasoned with treating ski injuries for many years. He is waiting for Mom in the exam room. Mom's blood pressure is through the roof as you might expect with such a trauma but her cognitive ability has returned reducing the concussion fears. Mom's blood pressure is usually well below average, except back when she was raising the five of us boys. So, they are having Mom stay for awhile, continuing to check blood pressure and oxygen saturation. Mom says her leg was hurting and pulled her ski sock down to reveal a Massive bruise welted up and covering most of her shin. A large odd shaped black mark near the middle seems to be the point where she may have been struck by a binding from one of the skis.

Then the doctor comes in to talk about options – we can go home and watch Mom carefully and wake her every three hours to check on her or go in for the CAT scan to check for any bleeding inside the head. He has seen a lot of ski injuries and thinks it unlikely and is recommending Mom go home. Dad asks the four of us boys. I vote for the doctor's recommendation, not wanting Mom to have to go through anything else. Everyone else votes for the CAT scan. Jeff calls Suzanne to get her thoughts and she insists Mom should get the CAT scan – the risk being that if there is a small bleed, it would take four to six hours to show symptoms and then be more problematic to resolve.

Mom, Dad, and my brother Greg head to the hospital
for the CAT scan. Hospital staff are waiting for them and
immediately get started. Within an hour or so they are
headed back to the house, Mom wearing a neck brace.
Results showed no bleeding in the head, but there was a
concern about damage to the neck ligaments. Many
additional hematomas had been found, all down the back
right side of her body – the point of impact. An MRI is
scheduled for Wednesday to check on the ligaments.

Back at the house, Mom is shaky but moving under her
own power. She settles on the chaise lounge as everyone
hovers to hug and talk to her. Mom's primary concern is
still that she is ruining everyone's vacation. We try to
convince her otherwise. Mom talks for a while and then
drifts off to sleep. Everyone is breathing a sigh of relief.

The next day Mom is up early with the rest of us and
has slept well. She is sore and still a bit shaky, moving
slow. Dad was already downstairs when Mom came down
and was a bit surprised when he went back up to find that
Mom had already made the bed before coming down. As
they are headed in for the MRI, Mom is still quite sore and
a bit shaky.

Results from the MRI are good, so they head out.
While driving back, they get a call from the hospital asking
them to come back for an X-ray to check for soft tissue
damage in Mom's neck. So, back to the hospital. Again

results are good, so they are again headed back when another call comes, this time from Dr. Wynn just calling to check on Mom, on his day off.

Mom and Dad head up to meet Marilyn, Dominic, and me at Deer Valley for lunch. We have a really nice time at lunch but Mom is having trouble keeping her eyes open as we are talking after the meal. Okay, maybe it was my boring conversation. Back at the house, Mom sleeps almost the rest of the afternoon. After dinner Dad makes an emotion-filled speech telling us how proud he is of Mom for being who she is, handling every moment with grace and true character. Dad went on to thank everyone there for all the support at the accident and after. Words came slowly as he told us how proud he is of his family; everyone chips in to get the job done, everyone gets along well, and everyone works well together.

I don't need to speculate on the reasons – I know why this is so – we were trained well by the leaders of the band.

Thursday morning Mom comes down without the neck brace. She tells us all she slept well and is feeling much better; the brightness in her eyes and lively conversation has returned – a thick gray cloud lifts from the whole group. Later, Mom said she had a dream about the accident and heard someone yelling "No, no, no." I tell Mom that it was Dad and I tell her about Dad calling after her as he skied down to her.

This Christmas we are reminded how truly fragile life is. Enjoy every moment with your family and friends and let nothing get in the way of that.

2012

There's a tendency to throw aside old values as belonging to an earlier generation. Don't discard those values that have proven, over the period of time, their value. Just believe in those values that made our nation great and keep them: faith, family, hard work, and, above all, freedom."

— President Ronald Reagan

Are you Smarter than a 4th Grader? - January 25, 2012

Sunday, the 39th anniversary of Roe v. Wade, Father Tom's homily was clear and unwavering on the subject. There was no room for discussion on what he might have meant, making it clear to all in attendance the church's teaching on the subject of abortion. For me, this was a welcome event as too many Catholics and non-Catholics believe that our church leaders are not united in opposition to abortion. For any that take a moment to listen to Catholic radio, AM 990, there is no doubt of the church's determined opposition to abortion.

We are gathered for our usual brunch after Mass discussing Father Tom's homily. He had mentioned 70 million babies had died from abortion in this country in these 39 years. A bigger number than I had heard before. Dominic, always eager to join in adult conversations, has that questioning face but can't find where to start.

I ask him, "Do you know what abortion is?" He says no. The words come out all on their own, "Abortion is when a woman does not want the baby that is inside her. The doctor takes it out, killing the baby. In this country, and in many countries, this is legal." Looking at no one in particular, Dominic says, "This should not be legal. No way this should be legal."

The wisdom of a nine-year-old—not even a moment's hesitation. My guess is that a survey of every nine-year-old on the planet would return exactly the same answer. It seems to me that much of the world is not as smart as a fourth grader. That which we treasure over everything else, our children, and nearly half the world thinks it is okay to kill them with abortion.

Later, thinking back on this conversation, I can't help but feel the sadness and outrage at not only having to explain an abortion to my nine-year-old but to have to admit to him that it is legal in this country. This country that I am so proud of for so many things; what are our children to think of us for having allowed this to happen.

There will come a day when future generations look on us as we look on Hitler and Stalin. They will see this as a time when this country and many others had no regard for life; allowing the most innocent and vulnerable to be put to death on a whim.

Freedom - February 16, 2012

Saturday afternoon I'm sitting in church watching Dominic's choir rehearsal and reading Matthew Kelly's "Rediscovering Catholicism." There is a discussion on the freedom that Christ gave us and my thoughts go to the freedom from sin that I had heard taught during Mass in past years – something that was always beyond my understanding. I love our Catholic faith and the peace that was Christ's gift to us, but I felt anything but free from sin. Knowing there are many things our human minds do not have the ability to grasp, I had taken it on faith as I do many mysteries of our faith.

For more than 25 years I was a closet smoker. Anyone who has been, or is now, a smoker knows this story. You know all the reasons to quit, and probably have quit many times, but smoking owns your life. There is never a time when you are not thinking about when you will be able to have your next cigarette. Even as you are smoking a cigarette, you will be thinking about when you will be able to have the next. This gets in the way of time with family and friends. An event or gathering where you may have to go too long without a cigarette will cause you to create reasons why you cannot attend.

For me, I had probably quit more than 30 times - sometimes for several months and sometimes for a few hours. Each time there was not an hour that went by that I did not want a cigarette, even after having not had a cigarette for many months. Eventually, you wear down and have that cigarette, and you remember how much you really enjoy smoking and then you are again a smoker. This is the insidious addiction of cigarettes; the physical addiction you can get past after a few tough days, but the mental addiction is always there.

Still, always I felt that I could do this, I could quit, I had a strong enough will. Then there came a time when prayer became a daily part of my life, and it occurs to me to ask God for help with this. Who knew? Again the first few days are tough and the first few weeks are hard to not smoke. But all along the way I thank God for helping me to not smoke that day and ask for his help to do the same again the next. After awhile I realize something has changed and I no longer think about smoking every hour of every day. What I could not do alone, I have done with God's help.

After having not smoked for awhile you begin to realize the freedom that is now yours. Smoking owned me and now it does not. I am free to live my life without being chained to a pack of cigarettes.

These many years later I believe that such is the Church's teaching on freedom from sin. When you are in it, it owns you. With the help of the Holy Spirit you can break free from it and have your life back and experience the true peace and happiness that was Christ's gift to us.

Since that time, as each Lenten season approaches, I spend some time in self-examination and choose something that needs fixing and go after it in the same way. If I live to be 100, there are not enough Lenten seasons left to fix everything that needs fixing. Yet I am thankful for each new freedom granted.

Blessings - March 10, 2012

Two years ago as all the second graders are in their final weeks preparing for First Communion, we are at church for the children to receive their First Reconciliation. We have more than 200 children in this year's class, so every gathering is a big group. Father Tom has a way of making this a special event and a special day for the children.

He recites a blessing for us, from Numbers 6:24, that God gave to Moses by which to bless his people. Occasionally the choir sings it before Communion at the 10:00 a.m. Mass. Father Tom invites all the parents to give their children this blessing every day from this day forward.

It is: "May the Lord bless and keep you, may He let his face shine upon, and be gracious to you, and give you his peace."

It takes awhile before my feeble mind can remember to do this every day, but eventually I get there. Most days all four of my children and son-in-law receive this blessing across the distance. Mornings when Dominic is at my house we sit in the La-Z-Boy and look out at the lake while he is waking up. Before we get up from the chair I give him this blessing.

This time sitting in the La-Z-Boy usually has the mind wandering in many directions. I wonder what the world will be like when my children are sitting in a La-Z-Boy with their children. Will this country still be the great model of freedom and liberty and opportunity? Will we have preserved that for our children?

I believe we will. This struggle over the HHS mandate, requiring all employers to cover contraceptives and abortion-inducing drugs illustrates how deeply we cherish religious liberty. Our Bishops have taken a strong stand on this, and there is a groundswell of support from many other groups. Even those that do not share our religious beliefs recognize this for what it is – taking away religious freedom, one piece at a time, and so they stand with us. May God bless them.

A simple question: What business does our government have telling employers that they must cover contraceptives and abortion-inducing drugs in their health plans? As an employer, is there any sanity in being forced to pay for drugs that cause abortions, or, even to be forced to pay for contraceptives?

Why is this something that the government should be meddling in? I've heard their arguments, and none hold water. After 236 years our government is trying to take away big chunks of religious freedom. You know that if they succeed in this the next step will be to force employers to cover abortions.

They will not succeed. We invite you to join with us in prayer and voice:

- Sign the Stop HHS petition at https://www.stophhs.com/
- Join us at noon on Friday 3/23/2012 in a nationwide rally to stand up for religious freedom – this is happening in over 100 cities. There will be some of us from St. Pat's going to the Howell location. Here is the link to find locations near you: http://standupforreligiousfreedom.com/ Also enclosed is the brochure for the Howell location.

Years from now you can tell your grandchildren how we all stood together to stop those in our government that would take away religious freedom in this country.

May God bless you and keep you, may He let his face shine upon you, and be gracious to you, and give you his peace.

Juanita - April 26, 2012

Marilyn's mother passed away Sunday morning March 25th. Marilyn had left my numbers with her sister Barb as she knew her mother's time was near and wanted to make sure she could be reached. Barb called as we were preparing brunch after the 10 a.m. Mass. Marilyn went home to pack her bags and headed to Manistee to be with her family.

Tuesday evening was the funeral home visitation, and Wednesday was the funeral. Juanita Berryhill was buried next to her husband. I had driven up to be with them after working a half day that Tuesday.

Their brother Robert had passed away in December, and it seemed this was the first I had seen much of Marilyn's family since then. Being with them through these couple of days there was much to admire in the conversation and the comfort they found together. They all cherished Juanita, and I know she enjoyed watching from above with love and pride.

Juanita raised eight children and two, Robert and Patty, had passed away before her. Patty had died from anorexia and Marilyn had told me a few times over the years how her mother somehow blamed herself. Robert had kept his illness secret from Juanita for a year and a half, fearing that knowledge of his fight with colon cancer would be too hard on their mother. Only when he knew the fight was lost did he let her know.

Such is the complicated relationship between parents and their children. Our relationship with God is much the same as the parent and child - the parent teaching, guiding, rejoicing in their joy, suffering their pain and always loving them as they are - the child wanting to please, yet often resisting the wisdom and guidance. It was when my older children were little I finally began to understand God's unconditional love for us – a parent's unconditional love for his children; God's unconditional love for us – it is probably as close as we can get to understanding.

Juanita served well her time here on earth, dedicating her life to her family. You can see her example lived out through her children and grandchildren. The words she heard as she left this world and joined the next - "Well done my good and faithful servant."

Walnuts and Watermelons - May 25, 2012

Most mornings we eat our breakfast at the kitchen island, Dominic reading one of his magazines and me the newspaper. A couple of weeks back he is reading a story about a guy sitting under a walnut tree looking out on a watermelon patch. The guy figures had it been up to him, he would have used the large branches of a tree to support fruit the size of a watermelon and left the skinny vines for such small things as a walnut.

Confident in his wisdom, sitting under this walnut tree, a walnut falls, landing on his head. Rethinking, it becomes clear that a watermelon falling from such a height may have killed him. The story finishes with the words "Allah knows best."

When Dominic asks who Allah is, I explain that God has been given many names and that the Muslim religion calls him Allah. Seeing the confusion, I continue explaining that Islam is a religion quite different from ours but interestingly their bible, called the Koran, includes much of the same books as the Old Testament in our Bible.

Dominic comments that his mom likes the New Testament better than the Old Testament. I say I can see why because the Old Testament has so many stories of such difficult times. Dominic asks, "Like Noah's Ark?" I say yes and go on retelling how God had used the flood to take all the evil people from the earth, saving only Noah's family, the last faithful on earth.

We had talked in our bible study how this did not end evil as it grew again after the flood from Noah's family and even Noah himself. We had speculated in our bible study group that perhaps this story is there so that we know evil cannot be ended by killing all the evil people.

Dominic is incredulous, "That's crazy. You're saying God killed all those people just to make a point?" I remind him that these were all very evil people and that perhaps the point is made so that all future people know that killing all the evil people solves nothing.

Dominic seemed to be trying to digest that thought and I did not have the words to take it further. How to tell a nine-year-old that the answer is in us and God working through us – teaching our children and bringing our neighbors along with us - while at the same time attempting to explain the complex balance inherent to protecting our family and our society from evil.

Those stories I hope are yet to come.

A Father's Day Tribute - June 16, 2012

Our Cub Scouts are now officially Webelos II with the crossover ceremony at Camp Dearborn. Much of this last year in Cub Scouts is preparing the boys for Boy Scouts. It is a time of learning to camp, learning about Boy Scouts, but most of all having some fun.

This is the time the boys find the reigns are being handed over to them. They are learning to plan and prepare for the events. They are learning to set up camp and cook.

They are building the confidence to do it on their own. And they get a little dirty once in a while.

We hear a collective cheer from the boys when we tell them as Boy Scouts they will camp and cook with their patrols, and not the parents. Being on a "real" campout we keep hearing "we need to do this more often" - a sentiment the parents hear and reflect upon.

In Boy Scouts, they learn how to lead, and they learn how to follow. They learn values, some rather significant skills, and become confident young men. Thus is the process of boys becoming men, when they learn to swim on their own and begin to choose their own path. An uneasy time for parents, a time filled with many emotions as they see this child growing up and wonder and worry the roads they will travel.

It is the foundation of parents and family, always there for them, that is the wind of courage in their sail to make their way in life. Later a wife and children add to that foundation and give them new purpose. Being divorced twice I have no credibility to comment on the husband and wife foundation and yet I know it is that and the children that drive us to be better than we were on our own.

Good times and life's achievements build confidence and self-reliance, but the difficult times are often what draw us back to God. It is there we learn to trust God and his plan for us, for working through us. It seems we cannot know his plan for us but we do know that all God expects is to give it our best every day. The rest we are allowed and expected to trust to him.

Christ's words to us, "Peace be with you. Peace is my gift to you." The peace that comes from trusting in him seems at times to be the best-kept secret on earth – hidden in plain sight – tell everyone about it, and keep telling them, and still it is lost on much of the world. True, it is very hard to trust in him if you don't talk to him. That would be prayer.

It was later in life I learned I could accomplish nothing on my own. It is only with God's grace that we accomplish anything. Nowadays I see God working for us and through us in many things, every day. My prayer every day, other than for all of you, is that God would help me to serve him today as he wants me to serve him.

We give our children many gifts; give them yet another – give them the gift of God in their life. They may not accept it today, may not understand it today, but keep giving it. My father and mother gave it to me and I would like to share it with all.

Happy Father's Day.

Am I a Man? - July 20, 2012

It is the Wednesday before Dominic's 10th birthday, and I'm heading to pick him up after work. I'm a little later than usual as it has been busy at work winding down the company and getting our brokers and their clients moved to another firm. Stress levels have been a bit higher than normal, but most everyone is pulling in the same direction, working towards the same end.

This quiet time eases off the day's pressures and allows time for prayer and the switch to life outside of work. During this drive, the realization comes that it has been awhile since I have been able to write one of these notes. The knowledge that I will be out of work soon seems to be getting in the way.

Picking up Dominic at his mom's house, he tells the tales of the day's adventures with his buddies Malcolm and Griffin. Hikes in the woods, climbing trees and jumping from a tree onto the trampoline were all part of the day's fun. He shows off his scratches from the tree climbing which you can barely see under all the accumulated dirt.

While starting dinner, Dominic is examining the long scratches on his arm and says that Malcolm and Griffin told him that you are a man when you get hurt and don't cry. His eyes are looking for my thoughts on the matter but he goes on – "I told them - Seriously? I've gotten hurt thousands of times and have not cried. I think being a man is more like when you are old enough to be out of college". Perhaps a bit of an exaggeration but he is a tough kid that rarely pauses more than a moment for injuries.

These are the conversations boys have with their buddies as they are growing up. I tell him, "Being a man has nothing to do with age. There are lots of guys well past college age that are still boys. Being a man is about responsibility." Dominic says, "I'm a lot more responsible than some people. Am I a man?" "You are nine years old," I tell him.

Dominic's wit being much quicker than mine retorts back instantly, "Oh, so age does matter in being a man." I tell him, "Being nine means you are allowed to be a kid. You are allowed to enjoy being a kid without having to take on any of the world's responsibilities and you don't have to be responsible for anyone but yourself."

I head to my room to change out of work clothes while the oven warms up and tears came to the eyes in gratitude to God for having given me this to write. It seems he is talking to us all the time – it is the listening that has always been the hard part for me.

Truth is that I have often joked that we are "guys" and so don't have to grow up and often I have heard wives include their husbands when mentioning how many children they have. It is the never letting go of "how to have fun" that invokes these remarks and it is the taking ownership of the responsibilities that God lays before us that makes us women and men.

Christmas in July - August 10, 2012

It is Sunday night, a little over a week since Dominic's 10th birthday. Dominic had lost a tooth today and there had been some discussion of the amount of money the tooth fairy leaves under the pillow. Dominic and I are saying goodbye to Marilyn as she is heading home. It is past his bedtime as we had stayed up late watching a movie. Marilyn had reminded him to put the tooth under his pillow.

As we are watching Marilyn walk to her car Dominic asks, "Dad, is it you that puts the money under the pillow?" "Yes," I answer. He pauses a moment and answers, "Well at least I can still believe in Santa Claus." Again a moment passes while we watch Marilyn get into her car and wait for her to drive off and he asks, "Dad, is it you that puts the presents under the tree?" "Yes," I answer. He answers, "I thought so."

As we head to his bedroom, I tell him "Dominic, it is your Mom and me that put presents under the tree, but Santa Claus is very real. Santa Claus is the spirit of Christmas that lives in all of us at Christmas time." Of course, this doesn't fit a 10-year-old's understanding of Santa Claus. I try to explain further but I fumble the explanation, and he is sleepy, so we settle to our evening prayer and sleep.

Come morning we are in the La-Z-Boy looking out at the lake – our usual morning routine as he wakes up. Dominic asks again about Santa Claus so I try again to explain about Santa Claus being the spirit of Christmas that lives in all of us at Christmas time – to find the words to tell him how it is this that makes it such a wonderful time of year.

I remind him, for perhaps the hundredth time that we are celebrating Jesus' birthday at Christmas. "I know Dad." "Yes." I tell him, "And this is why we give each other gifts; it is in celebration of Jesus' birthday. Jesus came to live among us and teach us. This is the greatest event that had ever happened on earth. It is Jesus' spirit, the Holy Spirit, that is the spirit of Christmas that lives in all of us at Christmas time. This is what makes Christmas such a happy time of the year."

True that many have forgotten why we celebrate Christmas and still they are filled with the spirit. God gives his grace whether we believe or not, whether we deserve or not, whether we ask or not. But, to recognize where it comes from is to truly rejoice in it.

When Dominic is older, I will tell him of these things as well.

We Invite You to Join - October 5, 2012

A few weeks back our Ambassador to Libya was among four people killed in an attack on our embassy in Libya. It was an apparent protest, turned violent, in response to an anti-Islam film produced in the United States. Spokesmen from Libya and other Arab countries were calling on the United States to arrest and punish the producer of the film.

This event and the views held by the protestors highlight the vast differences in our societies. We have that whole freedom of speech thing that other societies have difficulty understanding. Arresting someone for making a film makes no sense to us. We hold very dear a person's right to express their viewpoint. In the United States we would not get two people to stand in protest over an anti-religious film. Thankfully we have our churches, Catholic and Christian radio and TV, and even the mainstream media occasionally that take on the task of pointing out the myths and foibles in the anti-religion and anti-religious establishment films.

Stories of the protests seem to vary on how and why they started. Some of the protests, including the one in Libya appear to have been initiated by radical clerics calling their people to act. Do they somehow hope to make them stronger in their faith by bringing them to violence against a perceived enemy? My understanding is their

Quran has much of the same Old Testament as is in our Bibles. Isaiah 5:20 reads, "Woe to those that call evil good and good evil."

Seeing the influence held by the clerics in these countries causes me to lament the loss of morality in our country – the loss of influence by our religious leaders. On occasion I have wished that our Church taught more frequently and perhaps more emphatically the application of Catholic beliefs in our everyday life. In particular, when I hear reports that nearly 50% of Catholics vote for pro-abortion candidates over pro-life candidates – that could never be if they understood their Catholic faith and the candidate's agendas.

What if all Catholics heard the teaching of our Church and voted accordingly – we would have no pro-abortion politicians. We would have a country seen throughout the world as one that stood by its founding principles:

"We hold these truths to be self-evident, that all men are created equal, that they are endowed by their Creator with certain unalienable rights, that among these are Life…"

Last Saturday the Knights of Columbus were repainting the historic Chapel (built in 1840) across the street from St Patrick's. The Knights are a service organization and we have done several repair and maintenance projects on the chapel in the years since our council began. Always the conversations wander into many areas as we work alongside each other. Always the conversations drift to matters of faith and church. It is Catholic men sharing their views, their questions and their concerns with other Catholic men; some in quiet tones, some more emphatically. What a pleasure to be part of that. Then it is clear to me – none of these are among the 50% that vote for pro-abortion politicians. Nor is it the people we see in church every Sunday.

During Mass awhile back, Father Tom had asked us to each go and invite one person to return to weekly Mass. Not an easy task as we don't know who to invite, but, patience teaches us that opportunities do arise at times. If you are not a regular member at your church, I invite you back. If you don't have a church, I invite you to ours. St. Patrick's is an especially vibrant and welcoming parish. All are welcome. We invite you to join.

I also invite you to pass this on so that more are invited.

The Year is 2045 - October 14, 2012

It is spring and the year is 2045. Dominic's oldest daughter Elizabeth is back from college. Elizabeth is sitting on the porch with her head in her hands for a long while that morning. After breakfast dishes are done and things straightened up, Dominic steps out and takes a seat beside her.

Her face pointed at the ground, Elizabeth starts out slowly, "Dad, the other kids tell me I'm very lucky to be going to a university in Mexico. They say I come from a Third World country that cannot afford good universities. Is this true?" Dominic tells her, "Yes it is true, but it was not always so. There was a time when everyone came here for the best education." Elizabeth looks up at her dad, "What changed?"

"We lost our way. If you have a minute, I would like to tell you the story. I was ten years old when parts of Europe were collapsing under the weight of an excessive government that had created debts they could not repay and a government payroll they could no longer fund. Because they would not fix their own internal problems no one would lend to them anymore, even to refinance debts coming due. They would elect whoever promised them the most, regardless of how debilitating those promises were to their economy. In desperate attempts to continue their excess they taxed the industrious people so heavily they moved to other countries. Then each country fell into depression as its government ran out of money."

Elizabeth wonders out loud, "How could people let that happen? Still, we don't live in Europe so I'm not sure how that could have affected us." Dominic goes on, "There was a lesson to be learned from there and we missed it. Too many people in Europe had long ago decided that abortion was a good thing." Elizabeth holds up her hands in time-out, "Abortion?! What does that have to do with it?"

Dominic looks her in the eye, "Elizabeth, I know this is not easy to see or hear, but here it is – people kill their babies because they don't want to have to support the child – the baby they have on the way is inconvenient. They could carry it to term and let another family adopt it, but even the pregnancy is too inconvenient. So, they kill the baby before it is born. In the early years of legalization, people suffered huge regrets for having an abortion, many to the point they could not forgive themselves. Then over the years it became accepted and fewer and fewer knew regret."

Elizabeth starts to interrupt but Dominic continues, "Turns out when we no longer value life, when our babies - our most precious gift, become commodities to be kept or terminated, then we have lost our way and value nothing but our own comfort and security. Then we will vote for the politicians that promise us the most comfort and security for the least amount of our effort." Elizabeth looks skeptical but she is listening.

"When I was ten we were at a crossroad. We had huge national debt that needed to be turned around. Abortion had been legal for 40 years and already half the people stood for it and not against. We had the most pro-abortion President ever to hold the office, and we had a pro-life candidate opposing. The pro-abortion President was all about taxing the most industrious people and providing more government and more government benefits. The pro-life candidate believed in people making their own way, keeping government and government assistance down to the essentials."

"We re-elected the President, but still we could easily have reversed and overcome these policies when people saw what was happening. Instead many things happened to silence those that would have spoken up. First they attacked religious liberty trying to force us to pay for health insurance that included paying for abortion-inducing drugs. They called it the HHS mandate. Many refused and were served Massive fines. When they refused the fines they shut their businesses, first with the courts and then with force."

"Then they began to call us extremists and radicals – anyone that spoke up for conservative values, especially anyone that spoke against abortion. First it was the pro-abortion groups and then it was our own government, our elected officials in Washington calling us extremists and radicals. Then the media picks up on it. Tentatively they begin to report on others using these terms for us. Soon it becomes normal for every Right-To-Life group to be referred to on air as 'The extremist group …'"

"Elizabeth, do you remember that book I read from all the time." Elizabeth asks, "Your Bible?" "Yes," Dominic says, "Look at Isaiah 5:20 - *Woe to those who call evil good and good evil.* It is embedded in a chapter that speaks of just this situation we found ourselves."

"Next they took away our freedom of speech. It became a crime to speak openly of the things we believe. They called it hate speech. If we spoke against abortion, we were inciting violence against abortion mills. If we spoke of marriage being between one man and one woman, we were inciting violence against gay people. At the time the new laws seemed so preposterous that no serious effort was set against them. Then it began - they jailed any clergy that spoke of these from the pulpit. Next they jailed anyone that would write or speak out publicly on these."

Elizabeth interrupted again, "Dad, these are all bad things but how could that turn us into a Third World country?" Now it was Dominic looking at the floor as he answered, "No one would speak up anymore. The vocal had been silenced. So then we no longer had candidates that stood for conservative values – how could they get elected? No one would speak for them and they could not preach their own values – it was now against the law."

Elizabeth stares off into the distance and says, "So then the only way to get elected was to promise more to the people than the other candidate?! People could no longer get elected based on where they stood, or what plans they had to keep our nation on the right path?"

Dominic puts his hands on his daughter's shoulders, "Now Elizabeth, you have eyes that see and ears that hear."

I Can't Go Back - November 11, 2012

Dominic's school sponsored two Lego Robotics teams for the annual competition. These 24 kids, along with teachers and coaches spent many evenings after school and many recess hours building and programming their robots and practicing the missions.

Last Saturday was the regional competition in Sterling Heights – 32 fifth grade teams if I remember correctly. An all day event going from 7:30 a.m. to a little after four in the afternoon; many of the parents were a bit weary near the end.

Their robots performed well but our teams didn't win any of the robotics awards. But, they did win first and second place team spirit awards and first place in presentation. It's one of those things that "you had to be there" to see how these kids won the first and second place spirit awards. They rocked the place.

From the moment the competition began until the last award was handed out, these kids cheered their teams and danced and partied. Never tiring, never sad for more than a moment when their scores weren't on top - eventually drawing the other teams into it such that the entire gym floor was filled with dancing fifth graders. A great day.

During dinner that evening, Dominic and I are reliving the day for Marilyn. Dominic takes on a serious look and wonders out loud what recess will be like come Monday. He says, "I don't want to go back." We ask, "back to what?" Dominic explains that he doesn't want to go back to recess the way it was before Lego Robotics.

They have had such a great time working together during recess that he doesn't want to go back to the same old recess hanging out with the "Broskies." Broskies being their word for their band of boys that play together at recess. I try to assure him that their friendships from Legos will carry over and that recess will be different for all of them.

Dominic found something better and doesn't want to let go. Life is like that; we find something better and there is no going back. Faith is like that; you bring God into your life and you can't go back.

Faith is a journey lived every day, renewed every day. Mine started on the road back when my older kids were very young. There have been many ups and downs - filled with so many failings only to be lifted up again with God's forgiveness and patience. These later years beginning to understand what God expects of us, of me, and at last learning to trust him. Trusting in him is to then see God's hand in all things every day.

Towards the end of John, chapter six, Jesus is explaining the Eucharistic celebration that will follow the Resurrection. The words are difficult and those lacking a strong belief withdrew leaving Jesus and the 12. Jesus looks at the 12 and asks "Will you also go away?" Peter replies "Lord, to whom shall we go. You have the words of eternal life."

And so it is now – we have nowhere else to go. No one else to turn to. We have something better now and cannot go back. On this day of Thanksgiving, I am deeply thankful for that.

May God bless you and keep you and may you have a joyous Thanksgiving.

Looking at the Universe - December 15, 2012

An email to the family from my dad read:

"What happens when you point the Hubble at 'nothing'? It is hard to fathom, but planet Earth and everything on, and in it, doesn't amount to a speck of dust in the universe scale. [Then] Why do we get so uptight about an election every two to four years when the universe is measured in billions of light years?

Here is what happened when astronomers pointed the Hubble Space Telescope at what appeared to be [boringly] absolutely nothing, and left it there for 10 days; and, then again for 11 days. They then made the images into a 3-D presentation" (http://www.flixxy.com/hubble-ultra-deep-field-3d.htm). What started out to be "boring" became absolutely amazing!

I replied and forwarded it adding the below note:

Dominic and I found a moment this morning to sit and watch this together. They mention in the video that there are over one hundred billion galaxies and a galaxy contains hundreds of billions of stars. That computes to millions of trillions of solar systems. We are just one.

Makes me feel very small.

Saying it with numbers, we are one among more than 1,000,000,000,000,000,000,000. And this is only a guess based on what they can see with this amazing telescope. Perhaps it really does go on infinitely, and it is just that our beloved scientists feel duty bound to put numbers on things.

I asked Dominic where he thought all of these billions of galaxies came from. "God made them" was his answer. A simple truth easily forgotten; easily glossed over.

This month we celebrate God's gift to us. With all of the universe out there, God took the time to care about us, and bless us, and be among us always.

Makes me feel not so very small. So it is now time to welcome Him and thank Him.

Merry Christmas and may the Lord bless and keep you.

360 Degree Scanning - Conception to Birth – December 29, 2012

My dad sent the below link to the family with the message "Thru 2012 technology you can appreciate the miracle of birth. Nine minutes of magic...Dad...Grandpa."

I replied and forwarded it with the below note:

It is the days after Christmas when we finally have some time to relax and celebrate Jesus' birth. My dad had sent this to us and I'm hoping all of you will have a moment to watch. I have seen a number of inspirational videos, but this is extraordinary.

This guy, Alexander Tsiaras, marvels at the images he has put together using technologies that are presently in development. As he explains the precision and perfection of the baby's development, he concludes that only divinity could have designed this. I had a sense it was a glimpse into the essence of creation.

Please see this link for the video:
Alexander Tsiaras: Conception to birth -- visualized
https://www.youtube.com/embed/fKyljukBE70

There is a beating heart at four and a half weeks; at nine weeks there are perfect little feet and little hands. It occurs to me that if everyone watched this video it could end abortion forever. But we know that some will not be persuaded, no matter the evidence, no matter the weight of the argument.

In Winston Churchill's words:

"Men occasionally stumble over the truth, but most of them pick themselves up and hurry off as if nothing had happened."

In less subtle words – there will always be some that will not be persuaded regardless of a simple and undeniable truth right in front of them. They will drown the voice of truth with their own shouting - "and then pick themselves up and hurry off as if nothing had happened."

But some will be persuaded and then more. So please send this on to all your friends and family.

I was curious about who is this Alexander Tsiaras and found this bio on him:
http://dsc.discovery.com/tv-shows/curiosity/topics/alexander-tsiaras.htm

Merry Christmas and may the Lord bless and keep you.

2013

"To those who cite the First Amendment as reason for excluding God from more and more of our institutions and everyday life, may I just say: The First Amendment of the Constitution was not written to protect the people of this country from religious values; it was written to protect religious values from government tyranny."
-- President Ronald Reagan, March 15, 1982

Forgiveness - January 26, 2013

Monday morning Dominic and I are sitting in the La-Z-Boy looking out at the lake as he wakes up. It is two weeks past New Year, so the sun has not shown first light and the lake is all shadows and soft lights in the distance.

Like most mornings, I ask him if he slept well. He pauses a moment and then says no because he had woken and had been thinking about Evan. I ask, "Your cousin Evan?" Dominic answers, "Yes. Evan and I had been on a canoe ride with Uncle Jeff. Evan and I were in the front of the canoe. Evan was pushing, and when I pushed, he fell backwards and hit his head on the seat. I feel so bad." He continued trying to describe how Evan hurt his head and getting in trouble with Uncle Jeff for pushing Evan.

Having no recollection of the incident, I asked him, "Did this happen last summer?" He said, "No, it happened two or three years ago when I was seven or eight." I asked, "Could it have been a dream?" He said no that he remembered it clearly but then he had been dreaming about it. In his dream he was trying to hide, but still in the canoe the options for hiding weren't so good. Hiding by jumping in the water didn't work so well either.

Looking to calm his concerns I tell him, "Evan and Uncle Jeff forgave you long ago." Dominic answers, "I know; I just feel so bad for Evan." I go on, "The thing is, when we do something wrong the people we hurt forgive us, and, God forgives us. But, we also have to forgive ourselves. When we make a mistake it is important that we learn from it, but it is also important that we forgive ourselves."

We talk about him being the older kid and how he needs to be more careful when rough housing with Evan than with his buddies or older cousins. Dominic knows this and tells me so, but I am unable to pass up teachable moments. It seems that his dream may have been a lesson in facing up to our mistakes and so I mention that as well.

Perhaps it is in learning to forgive others that we learn to forgive ourselves. Guilt has shown itself to be a great teacher, but when the lesson is learned it is time to ask God to help us let go of it.

Of course we have all seen where ownership is not taken. There even seems to be a trend to deny personal responsibility – such an out-dated notion. Peace is elusive for them as guilt gnaws at the edges.

Forgiveness is God's gift to us and he wants all to share in it. Happiness belongs to those that own their mistakes, apologize, and then forgive themselves. Life is so much more without the anchor. Apologizing has another interesting consequence – it saves them from being burdened with a grudge against us.

Forgiving others lifts the weight of resentment from our shoulders - a burden so heavy as to hold us from moving. Yet we are prone to holding tight to these burdens when it is the letting go of them that gives us peace.

Perhaps it is in learning to forgive that we begin to understand God's forgiveness. Jesus told us, "Peace I leave you; my peace I give to you." Jesus came in sacrifice so that our sins would be forgiven and so it is that knowing God's forgiveness is to know peace.

May the Lord bless and keep you...

Leadership - March 20, 2013

Our first weekend in March was a busy one for Dominic. Saturday morning was the Cub Scout Blue & Gold banquet, then choir practice in the afternoon followed by singing at the special Mass for First Communion students.

Sunday we went to the Cathedral for the annual recognition Mass for Scouts that earned a Catholic religious emblem in 2012. Dominic and Keaton were there for having earned the Parvuli Dei (Children of God) emblem.

654 kids were recognized this year for having earned one of Scouting's Catholic religious emblems. Sunday evening was "Festival," the annual music student competition. Dominic received a perfect score again this year.

This year was our den's year to "Crossover" to Boy Scouts at the Blue & Gold. A big event for the boys, but I may have enjoyed it more than they. We've had some fun these last few years and have done some hard work.

Taking over the den a few years ago, it was my first time as a Den leader and I was a bit lost the first year. Fortunately, some of the other parents filled in the blanks to keep us moving. Interesting how you get attached to these boys and their success becomes so important to you. It felt pretty good having eight of them standing on the stage at Blue & Gold with their Arrow of Light award.

Five days after Blue & Gold is our first Thursday Boy Scout meeting. The boys seem excited to get started and are quickly gathered in by the older boys. As Boy Scouts, the boys are taking a step away from the parent leaders, doing more on their own and learning from the other boys.

Adult leaders are still the shepherds, but the boys learn leadership, values and quite a few skills as they are allowed to fail and succeed on their own. Failure teaches parts of the lesson that are easily glossed over by the success teacher.

Ralph and I are recruited to participate in a Board of Review - the final step for a Scout to earn their next rank. Hunter is up for earning First Class - a pivotal rank in Scouting. There are three parents for this Board of Review and we all sit down with Hunter to conduct the review.

We have a series of questions to ask Hunter relating to rank requirements, troop improvements, next steps, leadership and goals. Leadership being a key concept in Scouting – each Scout is required to hold a leadership position as part of their rank requirements. Here they learn that leadership is service and service is leadership.

On this question, Hunter tells us, "I would like to be a Patrol Leader again. I was our Patrol Leader early on, but then when my cousin became Patrol Leader, I saw that I could have done a better job. So I would like to try and use what I have learned."

There it was – my first Boy Scout meeting in more than a dozen years and I am presented with the reason for being here. It feels like an honor to be witness to a 13-year-old's awareness of his own growth. Reflecting on those words I recall it is the repeating of this process in all the boys that draws us to encourage our boys to Scouting and for parents to serve Scouting as adult leaders – many serve long after their boys have left Scouting.

There are those that would change Scouting for all its antiquated notions - that it's time to change with the times. I'm all for change as long as it means merit badges in technologies and such. But values do not change, and leadership does not change and service does not change.

Pointing to the example of our Church - the teachings to which we hold have not changed for 2,000 years. True, we have many failings as does anything run by man. But witness the world's attention on the election of our new Pope. There were a billion or so Catholics asking the Holy Spirit to guide the Cardinals in their voting. Non-Catholics also watch - perhaps for many there is solace in knowing that some things will never change. Perhaps for others it is just a curiosity.

I invite Scouting's leaders to consider the resilience of the Catholic Church. She has been here 2,000 years because the teachings to which she holds were given by God. Scouting has been here 100 years. It will be here for hundreds more if the leadership can see the wisdom in holding to core values.

In the Church, all are welcome, always. But not all can be appointed to positions of leadership or authority as adults. I ask you to join me in prayer to ask the Holy Spirit to guide all those voting this May to see the example and to keep Scouting on the right path.

May the Lord bless you and keep you.

Born and Unborn - May 4, 2013

Last night Marilyn and I sat down to watch TV after dinner dishes were done, a few minutes after 9:00. I turned on a Fox News show about an abortionist in Philadelphia on trial for the death of one woman and seven babies. Charges in the babies' deaths are for killing them after they were born.

We were watching only a few minutes when Marilyn looks at me and asks, "How is it that I have not heard of this?" After awhile, Dominic and his buddy Jake come in from outside and sit down to play some games on the iPad. We have to turn the show off so Jake and Dominic don't overhear this story as they are playing their game. Some things we should not have to explain to a 10 and an 11-year-old.

A former employee of the abortion clinic testified that the number of babies born alive and then murdered was in the hundreds. Another said the number was too many to be counted. Their testimony on the terribly unsanitary conditions at the clinic seems a faint whisper when the image occupying your mind is of a newborn baby's life being taken as it struggles to take its first few breaths – one of the babies born had been breathing for more than 20 minutes before being killed.

Kermit Gosnell is the abortionist's name, and his trial has been going on for the last several weeks. Many of you reading this are perhaps also thinking how could it be that you had not heard of this. That may be exactly the right question. Mainstream media loves to follow disasters and crime stories to such a magnitude that their audience finally grows weary of the story – so why not this story – a story that unfolded two years ago when the grand jury indictments were released?

Even President Obama would not comment on the trial; claiming he would not comment on an open investigation. Perhaps he did not want anyone comparing his views to those of Gosnell. When Mr. Obama was an Illinois state legislator, he worked to block legislation that would protect the life of a baby "accidentally" born during an attempted abortion. He had argued against this legislation and succeeded in blocking it – it seems that if the baby was not wanted it should be left alone to die – his words not mine.

Abortion supporters are often heard to say that abortion should be safe and rare. Yet they all indict themselves with the lie of this position as they endlessly fight any legislation to regulate the abortion industry – the very legislation written to protect women. To this day most abortion clinics are unregulated.

If the media were to cover the trial with any depth at all, it would have already brought into focus many issues with the abortion industry. Area hospitals had treated so many women for abortion complications that they repeatedly notified officials of problems with the clinic. For many years these notices were disregarded. If the media put a light on this, it could change the game. Hospitals would begin to consistently notify health officials of problems with abortion clinics and health officials would begin to actually do something about it.

Current status is that any action against an abortion clinic is frantically and loudly labeled as infringing on a woman's reproductive rights. The noise is so deafening it drowns out those trying to protect these women.

In Florida, March 29, 2013, a Planned Parenthood official testifies before the Florida legislature on the same type of legislation defeated in Illinois. Asked if the doctor should be required to care for a baby that is "accidentally" born during an attempted abortion, the Planned Parenthood official repeatedly says the decision should be between the mother and the doctor. Their word for this is post-birth abortion.

How could anyone defend such a position? But then how could anyone defend partial birth abortion? In my logic class from college days this is called begging the question. These questions beg the question, "How can you defend killing a baby once it can feel pain?" – 20 weeks. "How can you defend killing a baby once its heart is beating?" – 8 to 10 weeks.

The answer is there is no way to defend – they can only deflect, deny and disallow (shout down) questions of simple truth. Taking this to the end; even before attaching to its mother's womb it is clear that it is a baby, a human life created by God. And yet we find out that Gosnell is not alone. Turns out other abortion clinics across the country are also killing babies after they are born.

Abortion defenders have to defend every stage or their entire argument falls apart. Our mainstream media will not help us out on this. It was only after pro-life groups started email and Twitter campaigns that they gave any coverage at all to the Gosnell trial. They indict themselves for their failure to cover such a story. So it is on us to continue to pass the word; to speak courageously for the unborn; to deny anonymity to abortion providers; to speak simple truth to all, especially all abortion supporters.

Please, pass it on - ask others to be a part of it, to defend life.

… With liberty and justice for all, born and unborn.

Down by my Liver - May 15, 2013

Thursday morning Dominic is quietly getting ready for school. It is a few days before Mother's day. His morning routine is usually filled with song or chatter of some sort, so I should know to put my ears on when he is quiet. Stepping out of his room into the hall he looks at me and says, "My friend hurt my feelings yesterday."

When I ask what was it about Dominic hesitates and then says quietly, "Oh forget it." Perhaps he felt he should drop it because he knows I'm not too good with the whole "feelings" thing or it might have been that he was remembering our disagreement from the previous evening.

Dominic looks me in the eyes for a moment and then goes on. "I made them promise not to laugh when I told them something and they laughed anyway. I had a song stuck in my head but would not tell them what it was because I knew they would laugh at me. They promised not to, and then when I told them, two of them laughed out loud. They said 'fingers crossed' meaning they had not broken a promise. One did not; she was true to her promise."

Telling Dominic, "I remember getting my feelings hurt a lot of times when I was your age. I got pretty good at not letting it show so that no one knew my feelings were hurt."

We talked about how sometimes that is easy and sometimes not.

Puff the Magic Dragon was the song stuck in his head and then when he told them about the Davy Crockett song they laughed again. Both songs are assignments from his piano teacher. "Dominic, because you play the piano, you know a lot more music and a lot more about music than most of your friends." I tell him how those were both famous songs back in my day, that Peter, Paul, and Mary were famous folk singers that made Puff a popular song and that the Davy Crockett song was from a popular TV show.

Watching his face, it seems this bit of information is not going to help any. "A different way to say this to your friends might be that you have this song stuck in your head that was assigned by your piano teacher. Maybe even tell them you have a silly song assigned by your piano teacher and it is now stuck in your head."

We talk about being able to laugh at ourselves. I remind Dominic, "You are really good at seeing when things are funny and then laughing at yourself with everyone else." Dominic says, "I know, but it stills hurts a little. It still hurts a little bit down by my liver."

I think he said that to make me laugh but I'm not sure. As I drop him at his mom's, he hugs me and whispers,

"Thanks for telling me that stuff Dad." Driving away, I laugh out loud repeating, "Down by my liver." Those of you who know me well, know that there is frequently a delay before I see the humor in something.

Laughing at ourselves, by ourselves, lightens our load. Laughing at ourselves with others lightens their load. Taking ourselves too seriously weighs on us and those around us. Some days we are the light, some days we are the weight.

Jesus invited us to be the light of the world. We are to be the candle lit rather than curse the darkness. I think we are also to be the lift that helps others feel their burdens are light; a privilege to carry.

Matthew 11:30 reads, "For my yoke is easy and my burden is light." Jesus is telling us that his commands will not weigh us down. How could it weigh us down when he is always there sharing the load - many times through our family and friends.

Happy Mother's Day. May your burdens always be light.

Random Acts of Kindness - June 27, 2013

Monday after Dominic's last regular season game I'm in my usual weekday routine reading email while eating breakfast. There is a note from Coach Rob announcing our first playoff game on the coming Thursday.

A couple weeks before we had found out Dominic needed a minor surgery and as it turns out was scheduled for Thursday as well. There are few opportunities to get on the surgical calendar, and there was some urgency to getting it done, so postponing was not an option. I had neglected to tell the coaches about the surgery at Friday's game and sent a reply to let him know.

Wednesday morning, there is a note from Coach Rob asking if there is any chance to postpone the surgery so Dominic can finish the season with the team. Dominic is not one of the star players, so it is a touching request. I send him a note back to let him know that we will come to cheer the team on during the playoffs except that Dominic would probably not be able to come to the Thursday game since the surgery is the same day.

Coach Rob sends a note back Thursday morning at 6:04 a.m. to let me know that Dominic had been voted onto the All-Star Team which is why he wanted him to finish the season. He wanted Dominic to experience the All-Star Team - an act of kindness by a coach who cares about his players. Our team is fortunate to have these coaches – they are clear about what they expect from the boys but they keep it fun and give each boy opportunities at positions they want to play. Even letting the boys experience pitching or catching when the game outcome is still in the balance.

A couple hours later, on the way to the hospital, I tell Dominic his team voted him onto the All-Star Team. I wish I had not been driving so that I could have gotten a picture of his expression. Soon tears of gratitude filled his eyes. Dominic knows that he is not one of the best players and he was truly touched that the other boys voted for him.

Surgery goes well and I go to the game that evening. Pretty much every teammate wants to know, "Where is Dominic?" So I fill them in. Dominic is able to hobble into the Saturday game and everyone is glad to see him. Mrs. Gibson gives him a get well card signed by the entire team. Maybe it seems like a small thing to do but Dominic talked about that card most of the way home after the game.

Random acts of kindness? Perhaps, but I think this is who they are – these are kind people touching other lives when the occasion presents. Seems there is no way to adequately thank them for their kindness, but then they were not looking for thanks. Maybe it is enough to just tell the story so that others know the example.

One of my younger brothers, Jeff, retired recently and the company threw a retirement party. I could not attend but my mom told me about the many speeches given, and Jeff's kindness was a recurring theme. They were telling the story.

My daughter Katie and her husband Ryan decided they would be foster parents. Two little boys, Zeek and Jerrad, have been with them for the past couple of months. They stayed with me this last weekend and Katie and the two boys came to the 8:00 a.m. Mass with Marilyn and I. As usual, we run into several friends as we are leaving church and they all want to know who the two boys are. I could barely conceal how proud I was of Katie and Ryan as I told all of them that these beautiful boys are their foster children.

Zeek and Jerrad will be going back to their biological mom soon and are too young to appreciate or thank Katie and Ryan for the gift of themselves. But they didn't do it for the thanks, and so I am telling the story.

There are many other stories to tell but I think I have begged your patience with the length already. I admire so many for their consistent kindness – all of my kids, all of my family, friends, neighbors, and colleagues. Perhaps there will be an opportunity to tell their stories at another time.

St. Francis of Assisi called on us to "Preach the Gospel always and sometimes use words." And so it is with them.

May God bless you and keep you.

Zeek and Jerrad - August 8, 2013

At Christmas time Katie and Ryan told us they were planning to become foster parents and were going to begin the licensing process. I didn't give it a lot of thought at the time, but then I have little knowledge of the program or the process to become foster parents. Perhaps I could have asked more questions then, but sometimes I do heed the little voice that invites me to just listen.

I do know how much Katie and Ryan wanted kids of their own but God has not sent one their way. We had not really talked about it, but Becca, my son Ryan, and my son-in-law Ryan's parents would mention it periodically – seems these may not be easy things for daughters to talk about with their fathers. Yes, I have a son Ryan and son-in-law Ryan – sometimes makes it a little confusing in conversation and writing.

As Katie and Ryan were in the licensing process you could feel their eagerness growing. Answering their prayer, Zeek and Jerrad arrived at the end of March, shortly after they were approved. I'm not on Facebook, but my son Ryan told me the story of son-in-law Ryan's precious post about rocking the baby back to sleep in the middle of the night.

Jerrad arrives as a contented seven-month-old who rarely makes a noise. He didn't crawl or roll over yet, making it easy to keep track of him. His smile is quick and he loves to be held, but is also happy sitting and watching.

Zeek is a rambunctious three-year-old with a smile that steals hearts. He seems to love the whole world and gives hugs with the strength to interrupt your air supply. Like every three-year-old he wants to play with every toy in sight. Since their arrival, Zeek has been potty trained, and Jerrad has learned to crawl and pull himself up to standing.

Being on opposite sides of the state we don't get to spend a lot of time with the boys but try to make the most of each opportunity. I like watching Dominic playing with them and trying to be a 10-year-old uncle. I like spending time with them myself, reading books to playing in the water. Mostly I like watching Katie and Ryan becoming parents. They handle the boys with an admirable ease and share the load with humor and an affectionate nudge.

Occasionally we talked a little about the boys probably going back to their biological mom. It is a bit of a process that has lots of ups and downs before the court will grant a hearing for the mom's petition to get the boys back. Katie and Ryan's role is to just be mom and dad to them for the duration.

Soon after the boys had arrived, Zeek told them something that required Katie and Ryan to inquire with

Child Protective Services. Turns out it had been fully investigated a year prior. Zeek is three now and was two when the investigation occurred. There are more than a few possible explanations but still Zeek thinks it happened.

For several weekends the mom had the boys for weekend visits which is part of the process to qualify for a hearing to get the boys back. On the return from a recent visit, Zeek tells them of something that requires them to call Child Protective Services. They come in the middle of the night to see Zeek but he was too sleepy to give much of an explanation. They came again to interview Zeek but it seems he will only tell Katie and Ryan, so there is nothing more to be done with it.

In Matthew 18:10 we read, "See that you do not despise one of these little ones; for I tell you that in heaven their angels always behold the face of my Father who is in heaven." Jesus is telling his disciples of the guardian angels who will plead their child's case before the Father. It will not go well for a person to have an angel testify against them.

Parents live each day giving their best to serve and teach their children. They lose sleep hoping they have done all they could, or thinking they could have done better with this thing or the other. They pray for guidance for themselves and their children. When it is time for letting go they trust God knowing he will always be with them lighting their path and easing their pains.

It is often the purpose of the foster care program to give the children a good home until the biological parent(s) can demonstrate their capacity to be the parent(s). Last week was the hearing and the boys are now back with their mother. Our hearts go with them.

Please include Zeek and Jerrad and Katie and Ryan in your prayers.

God Bless.

Where is Everybody - November 1, 2013

It is Wednesday night, the first week at the new job and I am a bit late picking up Dominic at his mom's. I tell him about an exhibit at the chapel at St. Mary's hoping to convince him that this is a good way to spend our Wednesday evening.

Lori, one of the people in our Bible study group, had sent a note pointing out an article in the church bulletin about the Eucharistic Miracles display at the chapel at St. Mary's. It was put together by the Vatican and loaned out to parishes. I wanted to see it, and I wanted Dominic to see it as well.

St. Mary's has a large campus and I was not sure I could find the chapel, but there were signs directing us to the exhibit. We parked in the closest lot which was beginning to empty as people were leaving another building; kids carrying large sports bags which I guessed were filled with hockey gear.

We walked across the street to the chapel. It was about 7:00 p.m. and with no lights on in the vestibule it was dark inside. We wandered around a bit till we found enough light switches to light the displays and then started reading.

Each Eucharistic Miracle was beautifully described and illustrated on a large board. We kept calling to each other as we read one story after another. Some of the miracles appeared to have been specifically for someone that doubted the real presence of Jesus in the Eucharist. There were stories of healings; stories of the host flying into the air and glowing before landing on the tongue; stories of the host bleeding; stories of the host turning to living human flesh; a story of the host taking on the image of Jesus; and many others. Some have physical evidence that exists today.

Following this note is a copy of a discussion on Eucharistic Miracles that was at the exhibit for people to take home. It is a concise note to help us understand the church's position on miracles.

I'm guessing there were more than two hundred displays around the chapel. Seems like a lot for a chapel except that this chapel is larger than many churches. It was getting close to 8:00 p.m., the designated closing time, and Dominic was making overtures to be done. We decided to say a prayer of thanks before leaving. Walking to the front of the chapel, we are admiring the Massive crucifix and the larger than life wood sculptures of Jesus and the 11 apostles remaining with him at the last supper.

As we are leaving and turning out the lights Dominic asks, "Where is everybody?" Good question. I had expected a crowd as well but instead tell him that the exhibit has been here for a week and a half already so people have already been to see it plus it is a school night so most people stay in.

Sunday prior I was visiting with some fellow Knights in the hall waiting for the noon Mass to let out. Bob, a fellow Knight and member of our Bible study group, had invited me to lead the Rosary for the unborn after the noon Mass. Bob was selling tickets after each Mass for the Right-To-Life dinner hosted by the Knights. Our conversation turned to Mass attendance and we lamented the loss of attendance at St. Pat's. When I joined the Parish in the early 90s, the 10 AM Mass would be standing room only most Sundays. Now it seems we are a little more than half full.

Where is everybody? Perhaps our society has made it un-cool to attend Mass or to have a relationship with God (prayer). A person not strong in their faith can easily decide to put it away for awhile or just leave it behind. As for me, I look forward to Sundays, joining with neighbors in prayer and thanksgiving for our many blessings. Most Sundays the Mass is so powerful an experience I cannot keep back the tears of thanks. Dominic will sometimes ask, but he is accustomed to it now.

Looking around the church there are always many friends and acquaintances. These are happy people; you can see it in their faces. To recognize our blessings and to know

that all blessings are from God is to truly rejoice in them –
could be why so many seem to have a permanent smile.

If you are one of the many with the permanent smile, I
invite you to pass this note on in invitation to all. If you
have been away for awhile, I invite you to come back. If
you have never been, I invite you to join us. When you
come, introduce yourself.

If you would like to attend with someone, come with
us. If you don't live nearby, there are unlimited numbers
that would be glad to have you come with them. My
number and email are below if you would like to go with us
or if I can help find someone in your area for you to go
with. You will find us a welcoming bunch whether it is at
St. Pat's or any parish.

May God bless you and keep you.

Eucharistic Miracles Explained

The Real Presence Apostolate of Michigan answers some common questions about Eucharistic Miracles:

What is a Eucharistic Miracle?

A Eucharistic Miracle is some extraordinary event or phenomenon, which manifests the Real Presence of Jesus in the consecrated bread and wine in a way that we can discern with our ordinary senses. The manifestation may be as simple as a host floating on air, or as astonishing as a host becoming visible human flesh.

But I don't believe in Eucharistic miracles!

Our belief in Jesus' Real Presence in the Eucharist is based on Jesus' own words found in the Bible and on the lived Tradition of the Church. This is what we call public revelation. The Real Presence of Jesus in the Eucharist is a vital part of our faith. *Eucharistic miracles,* on the other hand, are not part of the public revelation and so are called private revelations. We are not bound to believe private revelations, even if officially recognized by the Church.

It is not their role to improve or complete Christ's definitive Revelation. However, they can help us to live by it more fully (CCC 67). Legitimate private revelations can contribute to a deeper understanding of the mysteries of our faith and to growth in our love for the Lord. Spiritual growth is an imperative for all Christians.

But are these legit?

Whenever a claim of a private revelation such as a Eucharistic miracle or an apparition is made, the church carries out a rigorous investigation. The revelation is only approved after the church is satisfied that (a) the people involved are credible (b) there is no natural or scientific explanation for the phenomena (c) the revelation contains nothing contrary to public revelation and (d) the revelation is leading to good fruits.

The miracles in this exhibition have gone through this process and are all church-approved. In fact, the exhibition was assembled by the Vatican to mark the Year of the Eucharist (Oct. 2004-Oct. 2005).

Why?

Many Christians, including some Catholics, do not believe in the Real Presence of Jesus in the Eucharist. In fact, this teaching is clearly supported by the Bible (see Jesus' promise of the Eucharist, Jn. 6; the institution narratives in Mt. 26: 26-28, Mk 14: 22-24, Lk 23:19-20; and warnings against abuse 1 Cor. 11: 27-29).

Some believe the mystery but do not grasp its implications or its dynamic power to impact their daily lives. Eucharistic miracles are a gift from God that recall us to the deeper meaning of this mystery of our faith. Pope John Paul II started his encyclical letter on the Eucharist, *Ecclesia de Eucharistia,* with the simple yet profound statement: "The Church draws her life from the Eucharist." Apart from Jesus, we can do nothing (John 15:5).

So, whether it is an honest day's work, playing with the kids at the park, leading family prayer, visiting the sick, feeding the poor, teaching RCIA, or rescuing babies from abortion, it is all possible because of Jesus. It is this same Jesus who is present in the Eucharist. So whether we realize it or not, the power of Jesus in the Eucharist enables us to live out our faith. The Catechism puts it this way: "the Eucharist is the sum and summary of our faith" (CCC 1327).

In *Ecclesia de Eucharistia,* the Holy Father reminds us: "Every commitment to holiness, every activity aimed at carrying out the Church's mission, every work of pastoral planning, must draw the strength it needs from the Eucharistic mystery and in turn be directed to that mystery as its culmination. In the Eucharist we have Jesus, we have his redemptive sacrifice, we have his resurrection, we have the gift of the Holy Spirit, we have adoration, obedience and love of the Father. Were we to disregard the Eucharist, how could we overcome our own deficiency?" (#60)

The importance of the Eucharist in our daily lives cannot be overstated. This exhibition can help reawaken or deepen our Eucharistic faith, draw us into a more intimate relationship with Jesus, and bring about a renewed commitment to, and enthusiasm and fervor to live our

Christian faith more dynamically as individuals and as the Body of Christ.

To learn more about the exhibition, or to help bring it to other parishes, schools, or organizations, visit www.rpamichigan.org

No Appointment Necessary - November 24, 2013

Two Sundays ago, after Mass and brunch, Dominic and I head to the Apple Store at 12 Oaks Mall. I can't remember the last time I went to the mall. It may have been a few years. Dominic comments as we are walking in that it has been years since he was at the mall.

With some help we find the store and are a bit surprised to see it is jammed with people. The parking lot would have you thinking the mall was maybe at 10%. I guess they are all in the Apple Store. Obviously, this is my first time here since everyone but us seems to know they are always jammed with people.

We have an appointment to have them take a look at our iPad that won't turn on and someone points us to the appropriate line. I had heard that appointments were required and Marilyn had bought the extended warranty so getting an appointment was easy. When it's our turn the guy asks a question or two and then takes about five seconds to turn on the iPad.

I had spent some hours on the Apple website trying their proposed solutions – all of which required it to be on. So I asked the guy how he did it and he showed me to press the Home and Wake buttons at the same time. Apparently this fixes the situation where it gets stuck between the wake and sleep stage. Mentioning that this is not on the website the guy says, "I know." Then mentioning that solutions on the website require the iPad to be on he again says, "I know."

Walking back to the car I mention to Dominic my surprise that a company like Apple didn't have that information on the website. Dominic says, "Maybe they just want people to come into the store." At eleven it seems he understands some things better than I.

Being the guy who always wants to fix things himself, I missed the idea they may be guiding people to get more of the Apple experience by bringing them into the store to fix their gadgets. Yes, you can fix some things on your own with the website support, but it is a different experience in the store.

I had always been a bit stubborn about being the guy who fixes things himself, including repairing my own brokenness. I'm one of those guys that pretty much kept everything to himself, avoiding talking things through with family or friends, much less talking them through with God. I was tough and could handle it on my own. Today I still struggle to be better at that. So it is that God gives us the grace to get through even when we don't ask. But he wants so much more for us.

He wants to bear our burdens and to share our joys; he wants us to talk with him. Parents feel this for their children and so perhaps more easily understand God's love. A parent's love for a child – God's love for us – so much the same and yet it is only the surface of God's love.

Some young people, trying to break free of their parents, might see it from the other side. Wanting to be free of rules, free of guidance, free to make bad choices; a child ignores their parents the same as we do God. Like parents, he is there always waiting our return.

Prayer is always there for us but he also wants to bring us into the store to experience him along with our friends and neighbors. Perhaps it is one thought on why there is suffering in the world – it draws us to him for healing. It is in our brokenness that we turn to him and ask him to help us through. It is in our brokenness that we can truly feel his healing touch. It is when we can sense that he is also helping us through the people he has put in our lives.

In prayer and in church we find all manner of new things that he has in mind for us. We need only be still and listen to his gentle touch. Each of us comes with a lifetime warranty and so he always welcomes us into his Church for any repair work needed; no appointment necessary.

Last evening, we were sitting in the pew going over the readings before the 5:00 p.m. Mass. Near the end of the Gospel reading, Luke 23:42, one of the criminals on the cross next to Jesus asked: "Jesus, remember me when you come into your kingdom." Dominic begins singing the verse softly. It is a verse we hear sung on occasion during Mass. I sing it with him a couple times than say, "Now you know where it comes from."

Dominic says, "Wouldn't it be cool to be able to talk to Jesus." I tell him that Jesus wants us to talk to him all the time in prayer. Dominic says, "I knew you were going to say that, but I meant the physical Jesus standing in front of us." I tell him that I know what he meant but as I had been working on this note for the last week and a half, I went on to re-tell the above discussion.

When I was finished Dominic said, "If the physical Jesus was standing in front of us, I would be pretty nervous." I agree, and in my heart I hope that I am ready when the time comes and I pray for each of you every day that he will bless your life and that you will be ready when it is your time as well. I want to be there, but more than that I want all of you there with me.

My dad had recently sent the book "*Surrender*", by Fr. Larry Richards, to my brothers and me. Enclosed was a beautiful note expressing the same hopes. Join us in prayer and in the Church doing all we can to help everyone's path to heaven.

May the Lord bless and keep you, may He let his face shine upon you, and give you his peace.

The Spirit of Christmas - December 7, 2013

Our Weber family Thanksgiving tradition is to celebrate on the Saturday after Thanksgiving. This allows my brothers and me to go to the in-laws with our families on Thanksgiving Day. It is a tradition started many years ago by my parents. In their younger days they were required to have two turkey dinners on the same day when their parents were still living in Cincinnati. This is at least part of the reason we celebrate on Saturday. We have so much to be thankful for that it should be celebrated twice, just not twice on the same day.

This year we are at Brian's house, my youngest brother. As my dad reminded me, this is a year I have much to be thankful for. My daughter Katie and her husband Ryan have a baby girl, Grace. They are in the process of adopting her, and they have a foster son, Kamren. My son Ryan and his girlfriend Megan are having a baby boy in a couple weeks. I do pray that they will choose to marry soon, but I cannot help but be excited for them, and of course to have another grandchild. Then I got a job in October after having been unemployed for more than eight months. Two grandchildren, a foster grandchild, and a new job is a lot to be thankful for.

A couple weeks' prior, Katie and Ryan had mentioned that Kamren had never heard of Santa Claus. He is three so it could be he just didn't remember from last year. They have had him only a few months and there is not much history detail.

At dinner there are three tables to accommodate the twenty some people. Grace is sleeping in the other room. Katie, Ryan, Kamren, and Dominic are seated at the table next to where I am sitting. Conversations can be loud with that many people so you typically wouldn't catch any of the topics at the other tables.

I can see Dominic talking to Kamren for what seems to be a long conversation. Kamren, as always, is more intent on eating than listening. Periodically I catch bits of Dominic's conversation – he is explaining to Kamren about Santa Claus.

There he is joyfully explaining Santa Claus in what appears to be enough detail that it must include the full legend from one of the movies. As the realization sets in, I am very proud of Dominic at that moment. It is the same as I feel about Katie and Ryan as I watch them being parents.

I have seen that pride in my brother Jeff's and his wife Marilyn's eyes as they watch their kids being parents. I have seen that in my parents' eyes as well. I imagine it is much the same as God feels about us when he sees good works being done out of love.

Is it the right thing to do to teach Kamren about Santa Claus when he might be back with his mother this time next year? Yes, it is. Santa Claus is the spirit of Christmas that lives in all of us. It is the Holy Spirit come to bring rejoicing in our hearts during the time we celebrate Jesus' birth. It is on us to spread the news.

In John 14:26 Jesus promises the Holy Spirit to his apostles and to us: "But the Counselor, the Holy Spirit, whom the Father will send in my name, he will teach you all things, and bring to your remembrance all that I have said to you. Peace I leave with you; my peace I give to you…"

If Kamren does return to his mother at some point, he will be a different child than the one who came into our lives late this summer. Perhaps it will be Kamren that brings the spirit of Christmas into his mother's home.

Merry, Merry Christmas.

Teachable Moments - December 31, 2013

Thursday morning after Christmas, Dominic and I are having breakfast. We are both excited for the day – Marilyn, Dominic, and I are having Christmas today for all of my older kids and their families. Katie and Ryan will be here with Kamren and Grace. Becca is coming with Ryan and Megan and Bastion. Dominic loves being an uncle and I love being a grandpa. We both can hardly wait for the little ones to get here.

He is seated at the counter and I am eating while unloading the dishwasher. Dominic is regaling me with stories of the TV show "Psych." It is his favorite show, and his mom had given him some DVDs of the show for Christmas.

If you haven't seen it, it is about a guy pretending to by psychic so he can get work with the police department. His photographic memory and ability to connect the dots are his real skills.

There is a pause in the storytelling and then Dominic says, "Dad, without going into a long story about God and all; do you believe in psychics?" I say "No." He tells me, "You are like the Lassie guy." Apparently this is the skeptic on the show that does not believe in psychic powers.

Teachable moments are rare and irresistible. Dominic has been subjected to more than a few which is why I think he prefaced the question with "…without going into a long story…" Lately, he seems to see them coming so I try a different approach. "Dominic, the Catholic Church instructs us to not seek out psychics and fortune tellers. Do you know why?" He answers, "Because that is going after false Gods."

I tell him, "Very good," and how proud I am of him that he knew the answer. I don't recall that I understood that when I was eleven. Adding some additional explanation, I tell him, "God wants us to trust him and his path for our life. We are not placing our trust in him if we need to know the outcome before God reveals it to us."

I ask him if he remembers where he learned that and he is not sure. I tell him that he must have been paying attention real well in Catechism and Dominic says, "and Church. You learn a lot in Church." I agree and tell him that I am very glad he pays attention. I walk over and kiss him on the head and give him a hug. The lesson is over. I wonder is it Dominic or me that has learned more.

1Chronicles 10:13-14 "So Saul died for his unfaithfulness; he was unfaithful to the Lord in that he did not keep the command of the Lord, and also consulted a medium, seeking guidance, and did not seek guidance from the Lord. Therefore, the Lord slew him and turned the kingdom over to David, the son of Jesse."

This was Saul, a king anointed by God, who had lost his way. When finally seeking help, he forgoes God's infinite mercy and turns away from God once again.

2014

"The greatest destroyer of peace is abortion because if a mother can kill her own child, what is left for me to kill you and you to kill me? There is nothing between." Mother Teresa

"Pray like everything depends on God. Work like everything depends on you." St. Ignatius Loyola

Righteous and Sinners - February 5, 2014

January 18, 2014, Dominic and I are going over the readings Saturday afternoon before his choir practice. Today there won't be time to read them between choir practice and 5:00 p.m. Mass – Marilyn and I have volunteered for the Children's Liturgy and Jill and Joe are going to show us the ropes before Mass.

At home, we like to read the scripture readings before Mass from the Laudate app because it has reflections on the readings. At church we read them from the MagnifiKid booklet – It is a kid's version of the Magnificat. My parents gave Dominic a subscription several years ago.

The first reading is from 1 Samuel 9:1-4, 17-19; 10:1. As we are reading, I ask Dominic if he had read the last note I had sent. He said yes he had, so I asked if he remembered the bible verse that talked about God taking Saul's life for being unfaithful. He said "Sort of," so I point out that this passage is where God had anointed Saul as King - interesting coincidence.

The Gospel reading is Mark 2:13-17. Many tax collectors and sinners had come to sit with Jesus at his house, and the Pharisees asked Jesus' disciples, "Why does he eat with tax collectors and sinners?" Jesus heard this and said to them, "Those who are well do not need a physician, but the sick do. I did not come to call the righteous but sinners."

Dominic wondered out loud who was more of a sinner; the righteous or the sinners. I tell him that righteous in the Bible means a person who does what God asks of us.

Realizing how incomplete my explanation had been before choir practice, I wanted to revisit the discussion. So I brought it up during dinner and we talked about it with Marilyn. We also talked about how we had realized during Mass that we had the wrong readings - turns out these were the readings for the Saturday daily Mass.

We talked about the word righteous and how it is a word seldom used these days. We might hear "self-righteous" which describes a person who thinks that they are holier and better than others. Much like the phrase "legend in their own time" describes a person who becomes legendary while they are still alive. Versus the phrase "legend in their own mind" which describes a person who thinks a bit too highly of themselves. Dominic asks me to not write about this in one of my notes because he would be embarrassed about misunderstanding the meaning.

Thinking about this later, I see it was me who had misunderstood. We are all sinners and so it is that Jesus came to call all of us. Dominic had asked the right question – in this reading the Pharisees were the righteous –

translated "self-righteous." In the practice of their religion the Pharisees separated themselves from any not like them and so could not understand why Jesus would associate with such people. Many of them also considered themselves to be holier and better than everyone else.

And so who was more of a sinner, the righteous or the sinner. Jesus was calling the Pharisees the same as he was the tax collectors and sinners, but so many of the Pharisees had ears that do not hear. And so again I learn from the student.

I tried to get in-touch with you today - February 20, 2014

I tried to get in touch with you today. We had not talked in awhile and I miss you. When we have time to talk, you feel my presence and the strength it gives you for the day ahead; all that holds you back is brushed away.

Since your day was starting out a bit rough, the sun came up soft and full of color to remind you of my love for you. During the night a new blanket of white was laid upon the earth to reveal the beauty in all things.

It made your morning drive a bit slower, but there were things we needed to talk about and it seemed a convenient time; however, the radio was on and you were bothered with the traffic. There was a chance during a moment you had turned the radio off, and then it was back on and you could not hear me.

There was a young man sent your way to bring my thoughts; still there were so many things that had to get done and there really wasn't time to talk. Later, another was sent your way hoping to find someone to talk through a problem. Thank you for listening and helping them sort things out. Interesting how our own problems fade when helping with another's.

On the drive home you were busy on the phone talking about your day, making plans for dinner and other coming events and we never found time to talk. Before dinner seemed like such a good time to gather everyone for a moment except the TV was on.

There was a sunset to remind you how much you mean to me. Bedtime seemed a good time to talk about your thoughts on the day and hopes for the next and then you were asleep too soon.

Sometimes you wake in the night when my help is needed. It is a quiet time when our thoughts can wander together. Many times it is just to bring perspective and ease the anxiety; other times it is to help with direction. On occasion you just need to feel my forgiveness. Resolution comes to view sooner when you understand it is me visiting, and then you are back to sleep. John 14:27 *"My peace I give to you"*.

Ours is a journey that will take time for you to know me. Each day is another chance to see how we work together. You are only asked to give your best every day and the rest you are allowed to trust in me. Some days will seem better than others and some days giving your best will be different from the day before. Remember, trust in me.

Such thoughts are not easy to understand and so a book has been written for you. There are many stories of the triumphs and failings of man, but it is mostly about my love for you. Come to my house on Sunday. There are men there who have been called to serve you and me; they read from the book and speak about how it works in your life.

Tomorrow there will be a bird and his song when it is time to wake; perhaps you will know it was from me. There may be some rain to bring the springtime to make all things new. Our talks will bring springtime to your soul and make you new again.

Revelation 21:5 *And he who sat upon the throne said "Behold, I make all things new."*

Tomorrow, and every day, my hope is to talk with you many times through the people sent your way and in the quiet moments we spend together. I will call again tomorrow, and every day, because you are mine and I want you to know me.

Jeremiah 1:5 *"Before I formed you in the womb, I knew you..."*

Holding a Grudge - March 28, 2014

St. Pat's has a children's liturgy during 5 p.m. Mass on Saturdays and 10 a.m. on Sundays. Children in grades three through six are invited to the chapel before the first scripture reading and return during the Offertory song. Awhile back there had been a request for adult leaders and Marilyn and I volunteered.

Sunday, February 23rd was our first time leading the children's liturgy. Leviticus 19:1-2 and 17-18 was our first reading and Matthew 5:38-48, the Gospel reading. Both focused on loving your neighbor and your enemies, not retaliating for wrongs against you and not holding grudges.

Such topics promoted a livelier discussion with the kids than I had anticipated. Their questions illustrate experiences with wrongs against them. We talked about how tempting it is to retaliate and how it aggravates bad feelings in everyone and solves nothing. Plus, it usually ends up with the person who retaliates is the one caught.

We talked about holding a grudge - how easy it is to hang onto that anger – how important that grudge becomes to us. Turns out, the person of our anger is usually not even aware we are holding a grudge. It is only making us unhappy and darkening our thoughts and our life. Interesting how much it lightens our load when we forgive wrongs against us – so much easier to move on with life.

There was a question about bullies, and we talked about simply telling them what they did was not nice and walk away; if they keep at it, then it is probably time to involve a teacher or parents. Easy advice when you are 59; but I didn't do so well with it when I was their age. So, we talk about how all these are not easy things to do, but it is what God is asking of us.

He is not asking only because it is the right thing to do, he is teaching us how to live a happier life. If we can avoid retaliating and have the courage to just speak to the person, then we come away so much stronger. If we can always let go our grudges, then we let go the darkness. Such is the difference it makes in your life.

Dominic took a moment to point out two things after Mass was over. First was there were a couple of kids giggling at each other across the room. Apparently I missed this but was flattered that he was annoyed with kids not paying attention. Second item was a process improvement to be remembered for the next session - seems other than that it was okay.

While shutting down the computer, the following Thursday morning, Dominic steps into the office doorway. We are about to head over to his mom's so he can catch the bus. Dominic says "Dad, that talk on not holding a grudge, that really changed me." I tell him I am glad of that. Heading out the door, asking about how it changed him, he talks about some situations and how he handled them. In the five-minute drive were told the endeavors of an eleven-year-old, holding onto guidance from scripture and working through how to put it to work in his life. I tell him how proud I am of him, but he probably didn't hear as we got out of the car.

If even a few more were so touched, I would be very glad – perhaps even one. Truth is, I am grateful that it touched even one - my son. I imagine it is the same with our priests and deacons – the effort required to prepare their words for the congregation without knowing how many will hear or understand. Still, they are there every Sunday with lessons prepared out of love for us. We are truly blessed with the priests and deacons that serve our parish.

A week earlier, working on one of my notes early Saturday morning, Dominic came into the office, climbs onto my lap and asked, "What are you doing?" I answered, "Writing one of my notes." For the last six months or so, I have included Dominic in the distribution list and before that would occasionally print one for him to read. He started reading and then scrolled up and down, and said, "You wrote a lot."

He scrolled to the top and started reading again. Dominic on my lap in the office chair, is not comfortable for either of us, so I got up and left him to read. After a time, he came out a couple of steps into the living room.

Seeing me, he looked off in the distance said, "Wow, that was powerful." There is no way to receive a compliment like that except to say, "I'm glad you liked it." The note had been in process for a few days but still needed work. Letting him know it may be several days before it is sent out, he agreed to read it again when it showed in his email.

It was the note titled "I tried to get in touch with you today." It was longer than usual as is this one. Still, some read it and to some it meant something. For that I am grateful. Starting out, these notes were written for my family and especially for my three older kids – trying to make up for where I was found lacking in a father's duty to his children's religious formation. Still, the notes are for them, but as time went on the courage came to include more people in the distribution.

One of the first notes talked about our faith being a journey and ended with a wish, "I hope that I have been, and will continue to be, a helping hand in any journey I can touch." So it is what is being asked of all of us – to be a part of each other's journey.

May the Lord bless and keep you, may He let his face shine upon you, and give you his peace.

Two Stories - April 15, 2014

September 7th, 2013. Saturday evening, I am headed to Kroger for some dinner items. It is a couple hours before the Michigan - Notre Dame game. My thoughts have wandered to my eldest child Katie and her husband, Ryan. A couple of weeks prior they had started the process to adopt a baby girl. She is not born yet, but they have decided on her name – it is Grace Elizabeth.

Their opportunity to adopt Grace came from a series of circumstances that seems a clear illustration of God's intercession - a gift to Katie and Ryan - a gift to Grace Elizabeth. To see it as God's work is to truly rejoice in it and to remind us to always trust in God. To see it as circumstance allows our imaginations to conceive all manner of fearful outcomes for the hurdles yet to come.

Becca, my second oldest, and I had lunch Friday, the day before, and spent much of it talking about their foster children and upcoming adoption. Here we are, two grown people having a pleasant conversation in a busy restaurant, with tears running down our faces. Seems it was a bit unsettling to the waitress.

Katie and Ryan had waited for our Labor Day weekend gathering to tell the whole family. It is also when we all got to meet Kamren, their new foster child. Kamren had a great time playing with all the kids.

Interrupting these thoughts enters a faint image in my mind of a husband and wife also waiting for the birth of a baby they want to adopt. I don't know the couple but I can feel their thoughts and feelings. Now something has gone wrong and the mother has decided to abort the child. The couple's pain overwhelms me and I hear myself saying, "Oh my God," out loud in the car.

The pain in my voice surprises me and changes the view from the couple to a man sitting on a street curb outside the clinic. His face is not visible as his head is bowed and the image is as distant and soft as the previous. His shoulders are shaking with his sobbing. Approaching I wonder if he is mourning for the husband and wife and the loss of their baby. Then I realize it is him and can feel the ache in his heart. He grieves with the husband and wife for the life he created. He grieves for the mother who will live with regret regardless that he has already forgiven her. He grieves for the father. He grieves for the child's life that would have touched so many others.

Again I hear myself saying, "Oh my God," out loud in the car and again the pain in my voice surprises me and shakes me out of the image. I am about half way to Kroger, which puts it at about three minutes since leaving the house, and a lot had passed through this feeble mind in those few minutes. Then I am trying to regain my composure before walking into Kroger, hoping the redness in my eyes will fade quickly.

Still shaken I say nothing to Marilyn when returning home. Later I know that I have to write this note but wonder if it can ever be sent out. It is an awful image paired in contrast with the gift He has given Katie and Ryan. Yet the image came to me in the same fashion as some of the previous notes and I can feel him with me; helping me write. Some of you know I do not have the creativity or the talent to write such notes on my own.

I expect that some may have stopped reading before this point, wondering how much I had to drink before that evening drive to Kroger. Perhaps even wondering what form of mental disorder would have me claiming the Holy Spirit plants the seeds and then helps me write these notes. The truth is the Holy Spirit is there helping all. We just have to be quiet and open to his gentle guidance.

James 1:5 reads, "If any of you lacks wisdom, let him ask God, who gives to all men generously and without reproaching, and it will be given to him. But let him ask in faith, with no doubting." Asking is now almost routine for me as these notes fail at the keyboard without his help. Still, each note is sent wrapped in the hope and prayer that I got it right.

Sunday afternoon, Marilyn and I went to join the Knights for dinner after their golf outing. Neither of us are golfers, but we do enjoy spending time with our fellow Knights of Columbus. Bob is sitting next to me and comments on a billboard he had seen recently – an expectant mom with the words "Adoption is an option." Interesting timing. Time was it was a popular option that seems to have faded a bit. I'm glad to hear it is being promoted again.

Two stories – one filled with gladness and God's blessings; the other only pain. Imagine what a different world this would be if the four thousand babies aborted every day were instead given to adopting parents. Perhaps then God would once more shed his grace on this country.

Addendum:

Saturday, April 12, 2014, Katie and Ryan received the papers finalizing the adoption of Grace Elizabeth. It is the day before Palm Sunday; a week before Easter Sunday. Grace has been with them since the day she was born and now she is officially theirs - a grand Easter present.

Revelation 21:5 And he who sat upon the throne said, "Behold, I make all things new."

This note was written before Grace was born on September 24, 2013 - I was unable to find the courage to send it until the adoption was final. For that I ask the Lord's forgiveness and yours.

There is another note coming that tells the story of how Grace came to them. It was originally written by my father and included in their Christmas card to friends and family. There is more to add now and I hope to be able to send it in a week or so.

God Bless.

The Path to Grace Elizabeth - April 23, 2014

It was the end of July when Zeek and Jerrad had gone back to their mother. They were Katie and Ryan's first foster children. Ryan was especially attached to Jerrad. We had been talking about the boys and Ryan said, "I still go to Jerrad's room sometimes and just sit for awhile." So many were the milestones passed in those five months that the memory fills a big space.

Katie told me they were planning to put their name in right away for more foster children. She said, "We feel that this is what we are to do." I have no words but now see more clearly the young woman who was once my little girl. And so it was that the Lord had in mind something more for them.

A 28-year-old woman finds herself homeless and pregnant with no job. She had found a couple to adopt her baby, but when the wife became pregnant they no longer wanted to adopt. A little more than a month before the due date she is trying to find a home for her baby. Telling her cousin the situation, he then tells her of a couple he knows.

Turns out her cousin Brett is the shop foreman for Katie and Ryan's company and he knows how much Katie and Ryan want children. They had not been able to have children of their own and so had decided to be foster parents. Zeek and Jerrad had been with them for about five months and then had Kamren for about a month before Brett came to see them about adopting his cousin's baby.

Katie and Ryan agree to adopt her baby, and Brett gives her a place to stay.

A few weeks before she was born, Katie was telling me of their opportunity to adopt Grace. They were more excited at the prospect than they let on; as was I. Right away there was a certainty inside that this was going to happen and they were going to have a daughter. Many ups and downs were yet to come, but nothing would change the outcome.

Telling the story to anyone who would listen, occasionally there would be words of caution in reply perhaps trying to help avoid anyone getting their hopes too high. My reply each time was to quietly say, "This is going to work out." There was even a nurse giving all manner of dire warnings as they spent time at the hospital waiting to take Grace home. They handled it well and just sent her away.

Katie and Ryan also handled well the drama of their several days in the hospital. Early on in their stay Ryan explained they are here to be supportive of the mother and tend to Grace. That changed in a moment when an event posed some risk to the intended path. On cue Ryan switched to family protector - Grace already owned his heart and he would stand in the breach.

Grace Elizabeth was born Sept 24, 2013, and Katie and Ryan took her home Thursday, Sept 26. Katie and Ryan were able to take Grace home from the hospital as they had already been through the licensing process to have foster children. Otherwise, it is uncertain where Grace would have gone on leaving the hospital.

Their foster son, Kamren, was excited to have a baby sister. They call her baby Gracie.

Perhaps all adoptions seem slow to the adopting parents and their family. Grace was no exception. Inquiries to the father went unanswered, requiring a prescribed number of attempts and time period. On the court date when the parents give up parental rights, the mother did as promised, giving up her rights and testifying that the father had made no effort to be involved in Grace's life – before or after she was born. Without her testimony it would have been difficult to end the father's parental rights.

Grace's mother is included in my prayers every day as are all of you. For all of her missteps, when it came to Grace she did the right thing, and she did what she said she would do. Katie told me that she had found a job and I hope that her life will take a new path. May God bless her.

It would be easy to attribute the path to Grace Elizabeth to circumstance except that there are so many other likely outcomes. God's gentle touch is there for us to see in many things every day. Here God has blessed Grace Elizabeth with Katie and Ryan, and Katie and Ryan with Grace Elizabeth.

My Country Tis of Thee... - September 3, 2014

In the Old Testament there was a time of kings when the people of Israel lived in the Promised Land. A man named Ahab was one of the kings in the ninth century BC. Ahab had been influenced by his wife Jezebel to worship Baal rather than the God of Israel. She convinced Ahab that Baal provided the rain and other needs of the land, but the lure that pulled in Ahab and so many others was the "anything goes" society.

Baal required sacrifice in order to provide for the people - human sacrifice and much of the time human children. So beguiled were the many followers, they willingly sacrificed their children and celebrated the events. Still there were not always enough, so in times of trouble the king made laws to require them from the prominent and wealthy families. Parents would watch as their children were burned alive on the altars of Baal. A great noise would be raised to drown the screams of anguish from the children and their parents.

God sent Elijah to bring the people back to him but they would not listen. Elijah held a contest to prove the impotence of Baal in the face of God and then many did return. But Ahab would not be convinced and his reign failed.

147

Part of the reason the early church grew so quickly was the martyrs. They believed in Jesus and no amount of government coercion would dissuade them. It was their willingness to die at the hands of their government, rather than deny their faith, that brought so many others into the faith. They kept teaching their faith up to the moment they died. In death they taught the world.

Those in this country willing to stand against the government include the owners of Hobby Lobby and Conestoga Wood, risking fines so crippling as to destroy their companies. They and 300 other companies and organizations sued our government to prevent enforcement of the HHS Mandate – part of the Affordable Care Act (ACA), also known as Obamacare. This HHS Mandate was the rules created by the HHS Department to force companies to provide free contraception, sterilization, and abortion-inducing drugs to their employees. These things go against the faith of Catholics and many other Christian denominations.

Much of the media tried to mock and humiliate them. They called it a "War on Women," claiming these companies were trying to prevent women's access to birth control. I find myself wanting to shout at the TV and news articles that suborn this deceit. Seems they must know that not wanting to pay for it is so different than preventing access. Especially since birth control is inexpensive and already free to many under existing government programs.

148

With the HHS Mandate taking effect in 2014, access to birth control did not change, and, voiding the HHS Mandate in the Supreme Court also did nothing to change access.

Of course the media ignored this and the whole concept of forcing companies to pay for abortion-inducing drugs. Think of the mockery it is to require an organization like Priests for Life to provide abortion-inducing drugs to their employees. Much of the time, companies are a reflection of the owners' personality. Who they are and what they stand for is evident even to the casual observer within. If our government can successfully force company owners to provide free abortion-inducing drugs, then they will have demeaned all industry leaders – not just men and women of faith.

Independence Day, 2014 will perhaps be remembered for turning back those that would take away the freedom of religion. An overreaching government tried to take away the right to carry our values and beliefs into the workplace. Led by the 300, many have come to see this law for the outrage that it was – it is the debate that makes transparent all the spin. And yet those in DC that produced this law are busy trying to write another – it will fail as well. They would have us worship at the altar of sexual freedom and force company owners to pay for it. And then raise a great noise to drown out the voices of dissent.

It is true that the HHS mandate had an exemption for organizations with the primary purpose of worship and teaching the faith - a very narrow exemption that essentially meant only churches. It seems to me that any coercive law that requires a "Religious Exemption" is inherently wrong and in opposition to our constitution and the great men and women who built this country. So it is that these religious exemptions are an obvious and vain attempt to placate.

We were supposed to forget who we are when we step out of our homes and out of our church. There is so much they don't understand. Our church is not a building; it is the people. We are never out of the church, we are always among fellow believers and God is always among us. Are we to deny what God has commanded – deny it in front of others; in front of God? We cannot because to do so is to deny our faith, to deny God.

I love our country, and I love our form of government. Sometimes the people in our government get it wrong. Fortunately, there are men and women with the courage to stand against. We all need to be part of that voice.

The victory was won by the narrowest of margins; perhaps coincidentally it happened at the beginning of the week we celebrate Independence Day. History is often made with such narrow margins. Our Supreme Court, by a vote of five to four, held that companies also have the right to religious liberty – the government cannot force the owners to do things that go against their faith.

God Bless America.

Coming Home - September 27, 2014

Saturday, September 13th, Katie and Ryan celebrated Kamren's fourth birthday at Chucky Cheese's. Kamren had a great time with all the rides and games and everything. They have had him for a little over a year now, and he is becoming a nice young man. Grace was having fun demonstrating her newfound walking skills.

Foster care is generally intended to give the biological parents' time to get their lives together in order to get their kids back. That didn't work for Kamren's biological parents and a judge terminated their parental rights on Tuesday, September 16th, 2014. It will take a few weeks for the termination paperwork to be registered in the system and then Katie and Ryan will be able to begin the adoption process. It is expected to take six to nine months, and it is a bit of a rollercoaster, so please keep Katie and Ryan and Kamren in your prayers.

Katie called me at work that Tuesday to tell me the news. There I was, pacing around my office, tears running down my face while talking on the phone with Katie. Just a year ago Grace was about to be born and they would begin the process to adopt her. Hers was final in April this year and now they start again with Kamren.

My ride home from work is generally 45 minutes to an hour or so and I use the time to say a rosary for all of you and then usually let my thoughts wander in the quiet time that remains. On this Tuesday, I recall some thoughts on Grace and Kamren coming into their life. Did our Lord bring them Grace and Kamren because they could not have children? Or was it that they could not have children because our Lord needed a home for Grace and Kamren?

I think the answer is yes to both. So it is to recognize God's hand in our lives is to truly rejoice in his blessings.

May the Lord bless and keep you, may He let his face shine upon you, and give you his peace.

Heart to Heart - October 24, 2014

Dominic called me at work on a Monday afternoon as he and his mom were on their way back from his Dr. Russell visit. Dominic had heart surgery when he was four days old to repair a condition known as Tetralogy of Fallot. Since then he has an annual visit with Dr. Russell to follow his progress. Each time there is an EKG and an Echocardiogram – one records the electrical impulses from the heart and the other is an ultrasound of the heart.

They had noticed his aorta was a bit enlarged in the last few visits and so had put him on a beta blocker last year to correct it. Also a few years ago, Dr. Russell had told us that when Dominic was in high school he would need a valve for his pulmonary artery and when he was 12 they would do an MRI to get a closer look. Part of his heart repair at birth involved losing the pulmonary artery valve.

Dominic told me that there was a change in plan and they were going to put the valve in next spring. Turns out the MRI showed an enlargement to his right ventricle and they want to put the valve in to prevent further enlargement. He told me all of this with the same cheerful voice he would tell me of a fun day at school. When I asked him if it bothered him, he replied, "I cried a little bit."

Mornings we sit in the La-Z-Boy and look out at the lake as he wakes up. Our time is much shorter now as he

154

has to catch the bus so early. Thursday morning, after the Dr. Russell visit, I ask Dominic to join me in a prayer. So after his blessing, we pray together, "Dear Lord, if it is your will, let this cup pass from this boy so that he may not have open heart surgery." We say this prayer every time we are together now and would be glad for you to join with us.

There is a very small chance they may be able to put the valve in via a catheter, but the technology is not there yet. We talked about this, and that we are lucky for him to be able to have this done at U of M – The University of Michigan, Mott Children's Hospital. They are the best in the world at repairing children's congenital heart defects and have pioneered many of the techniques used around the world. I asked him if he is worrying about it and he says no, that he really doesn't think much about it.

On a Sunday evening, a couple weeks later, I asked Dominic if he wanted to see the website I had put together of all my notes. He sits down to look at it on the iPad and browsed around for awhile. Just before we are about to sit down to dinner, he announces he is reading "Tears of Thanksgiving." Marilyn was about to call him to dinner and I said let's let him finish that one. It is the story of his first heart surgery.

Dominic had that far-off look on his face as he sat down. He had a couple of thoughts on the note that he wanted to share. First, it was tough to read because a certain part was so blunt. I told him it was not half as tough as being there. Second, he thought that I need not apologize to God for my lack of faith. Seems he thought my reaction was justified. We went on to talk about that and more about the note, sharing a fair number of tears and hugs during dinner.

Wednesday following, at dinner, I tell him I am planning to send out one of my notes about this and ask if he is okay with that. He gives me thumbs up and goes on to explain that he has been telling his friends and they have some questions he is not sure how to answer. Dominic asks, "Will I die if I don't have the surgery?" I don't know the answer either but we talk about how good these doctors are, and they know how to give you the best chance for a long and healthy life. We plan to ask these questions when we meet in May with Dr. Ohye, his heart surgeon.

Dominic has had three surgeries for other things in the 12 years after his heart surgery. Each time he approached it as just another thing to do – no fear, but taking a long look in my eyes just before going under. Perhaps looking for confidence in my eyes; perhaps hoping to not see fear. For several years he would occasionally recall the first one from when he was very little – "Dad, remember the uckie?" It was the smell of the mask they put over his face to put him out.

When our children are little, they trust in us completely. They also know about trusting in God because it is what we teach them, yet may not be sure what it means. As they grow they find out we are far from perfect, though it is also the time they are learning to rely more on themselves. Giving them the gift of trusting in God is to give them the confidence to tackle life's ups and downs and to rejoice in every step. Trusting in our Lord is to sit down with Him in prayer and then find Him with us on our journey.

If you would like to see the website, please see http: wordsfrommyfather.com. The note "Tears of Thanksgiving" is on the "Prior Years" page.

Celebrity Pictures - November 16, 2014

Last evening was the Save A Heart charity event. Save A Heart is the organization that helps families with travel, lodging and food costs when their child is at U of M for heart surgery and follow-up care. Children come from all over the world to U of M, and for some families, Save A Heart makes the difference whether they can afford to be there with their child.

This was Dominic's first time attending and it just so happened Devin Gardner, Michigan's quarterback, was at the event. We imposed on him for a picture with Dominic and his cousin Toni. He was very gracious. Later we saw Dr. Ohye, Dominic's heart surgeon, and I said to Dominic, "Let's get a picture with him." Dominic protested and I said, "Dominic, I would rather have a picture with Dr. Ohye than Devin Gardner." Dominic looked at me and said, "Really? Okay."

He knew how cool it was to have a picture with Devin Gardner and now he knew how much Dr. Ohye meant. Perhaps his fan base is a bit smaller, but he is a true celebrity to all the families whose children are alive today because of him and the team at U of M.

God Bless.

2015

"I have been driven many times upon my knees by the overwhelming conviction that I had nowhere else to go. My own wisdom, and that of all about me, seemed insufficient for that day."

- President Abraham Lincoln

Twelve Past One Hundred - February 1, 2015

Stories about my great-grandmother had been rolling around in my head in the weeks before Christmas and it was time to start writing. Mom and Dad were in town and I asked if they were okay with it before starting. A first draft went to them and to my Aunt Nancy and Uncle Tom. They helped sort out details and sent additional stories which are included - paraphrased a bit. All of this makes for a longer than usual note and so may take more than one sitting. I promise laughter and tears and perhaps an inspiring thought or two.

From Nancy:
Antoinette Massman was born January 22, 1880, at home. They lived in Correyville (part of Cincinnati). Each nationality had their area of town. She had two brothers, Bill (married Oylee) and Ted (married Thelma).

Before she was married, she worked as a seamstress downtown. Her Mama packed her lunch each day and sent her with enough money for one way on the trolley – she walked the other way. Her whole salary went to Mama. She told me that on Sundays they would take a nice walk and Mama would cook them a nice dinner.

She married Otto Huber and had four children and at some point move to Oakley. Our Dad, Oliver George was the oldest, born in 1904. Bert (Alberta) was next, then

Marvin and Billy. Marvin died at about eight years old from Diptheria - no vaccine then. He was laid out in his first Communion suit which Grandma made.

Billy was a late in life baby. Measles and Encephalitis caused mild retardation. These days he could have been educated and probably able to hold a job.

Grandpa gave her a treadle sewing machine for a wedding present. She loved to sew and treasured the sewing machine. She made Grandpa's suit for their wedding, and she made a dress for me that I truly loved. It was a summer dress with a matching bonnet, so I called it my bonnet dress. I can still picture it and remember that I could not understand when I had grown out of it. I wanted to wear it forever.

Mom also talked about Grandma making dresses for them:
She would often make dresses for Nancy and me for Christmas. Often the dresses were velvet.

From Nancy:
They always had a vegetable garden in the backyard and did a lot of canning. I loved her cooking – very tasty and nutritious and, being German, everything was spotless.

Grandma was strict and firm with us – not a Grandma to spoil grandchildren. I'm sure I was a pain in the neck -

she was always telling me to be quiet and would say I must have been vaccinated with a phonograph needle. Another subtle hint was, "Children should be seen and not heard." She definitely mellowed with age.

Back then there was some ill will between the German and Irish, and Grandma would occasionally make comments about the Irish. Of course my mother, being Irish, would not have been pleased. After Grandma was 100, she was asked to ride in the St. Patrick's Day Parade as the Grand Marshal and she was thrilled. She did Mellow as she aged.

Grandpa developed sores on his ankles and eventually lost both legs. He used crutches after the first leg. After the second Grandma pushed him in a wheelchair but he also made leather tubes with a round sole to fit each stump so he could get around a bit on his own using two short canes. Grandma pushed him in his wheelchair to church every day and would bring his lunch to him each noontime at his shoe shop.

At some point, Billy moved into a group home in Kentucky that was run by a priest and Catholic Brothers. In the early 70s Billy died. Grandma said her prayers were answered...she wanted to know he was taken care of before she died.

Grandma always lived on the second floor of her apartments because it was less expensive. At a certain age, parishioners insisted on picking her up in a car to take her to church. She would laugh and say, "They think I am old."

Every year around her Birthday, after she was 100, the city newspaper would interview her. They asked her once, what was the oldest thing in her apartment and she said, "Me of course."

Maybe at about 90, she fell and broke her collar bone. The worse part by her standards was she couldn't fit regular dresses on and had to wear a "housecoat." Apparently proper ladies did not wear housecoats.

When she worked in her garden, she always wore a hat and long-sleeved dresses - didn't want ANY tan. Apparently, proper ladies also did not get tan.

When Tom and I were dating, and he was 18 or 19, Grandma had the family over for a Sunday dinner - Sue, Bert, our family and maybe Aunt Olyee. Grandma asked Tom to help her get a pillow out from UNDER the sofa-bed. It was a booster for Sue to sit on at the table. Before Tom could get over there, she had the sofa in the air, motioning him to get the pillow out! A little later, the doorbell rang, and Grandma beat Tom downstairs to open the door. He was mortified about this little old lady beating him to the punch. At the time he said he would never be able to look her in the eye.

Because she was such a walker, Tom used to kid her asking when she was going to walk to Indianapolis to visit us. She enjoyed people kidding her.

Bishop Bernadin, who later became a Cardinal and the Archbishop of Chicago, said Mass at St. Cecelia's Church for her 100th birthday. It was televised by a local TV Station and shown on the News. At the party in the Church Hall after the Mass, she stood on a table so everyone could see her. She really looked good at that age.

My first memories of Great Grandma were probably when she was in her early to mid-80's; about the age my parents are now. She lived in a small house in Cincinnati, and we would visit her during our annual trip. She always had a bunch of pennies on top of her dresser that she would divide up between my brothers and me.

grand daughter Nancy, great grandma, daughter, Bert, grand daughter Sue, grand daughter Betty (my mother)   1986 - 107th birthday

When she turned 99, the extended family went for her birthday and every birthday after until her last at 112. There was always a large group and everyone took time to talk with Great Grandma. She remembered all of us and loved talking to everyone. It was only in the last year or two that failing eyesight and hearing required her a moment or two to recognize each person.

About the time I was in high school or college, we were talking about how Great Grandma always recognized everyone immediately; saying their name as she grabbed their hand with both of hers. Dad explained that she prayed the rosary for all of us every day, reciting each of our names as she began. Mom and Dad occasionally mentioned the blessings flowing to our family and to all of Great Grandma's family from her daily rosary. Perhaps all of us have little idea of the people praying for us and easily take for granted the blessings in our lives.

She and her daughter Bert would come up to Michigan for various family events. When Katie, my oldest, was a baby they went with us to Sunday morning Mass at Our Lady of Sorrows. The assistant pastor paused at our pew to say hi and I introduced everyone. When I told him she was 101, he became very excited, explaining he had never met anyone that was over 100 years old. He rushed off to find a gift for her returning with a fancy loaf of bread. Great Grandma held his hand for a moment as she thanked him.

Great Grandma's husband, Otto, was a shoemaker, which became a shoe repair business when store-bought shoes became popular. He had lost his legs to diabetes and Great Grandma would push him around town in his wheelchair. She also walked all over to pick up and deliver shoes. Neither of them drove a car. He passed away in the spring of 1948, around age 70, and Great Grandma continued to support herself working in the plant at the American Playing Card Company. It was close enough for her to walk.

They did not have much money so Great Grandma made arrangements to pay for his funeral and burial with monthly payments. The funeral home was quite a distance, but she made the trip every month to deliver the payment. After some time, the owner, not wanting her to make the journey each month, told her it was paid in full. She told him she knew how much she still owed and would be back every month until it was paid.

Great Grandma was pretty tough and the owner could see there was no point in debate, so instead he told her very well, but when it is your time I will do your funeral for free. Of course one of the things that comes with living to 112 is you outlive your friends and the owner of the funeral home. Still, his children honored the promise.

Heather talking to great grandma on her 111th birthday. 1990

Outliving friends is hard on a person, but then Great Grandma also outlived three of her four children. At my grandfather's funeral Great Grandma was standing by the casket looking at her son. Tears on her face, but in a firm voice, she said, "A parent should not have to outlive her children."

With four children and three grandchildren of my own, that thought echoes in my mind and brings tears to my eyes every time I tell the story. It seemed she was angry when she said it and I wondered if she was angry at God. She loves God so much I'm guessing it was not directed at God – perhaps she just needed to recognize her anger so she could let go of it. As it was that Mary had to bury her only child, I believe that she has a particular regard for all parents that have lost a child and intercedes with our Lord to give them the grace to weather the loss.

We all enjoyed Great Grandma's sense of humor and she seemed to enjoy laughing at herself more than anything. On one trip we picked her up for her birthday party. She bumped her head on the door frame as she was getting out of the van and the thump was loud enough to make me cringe and move quickly towards her to help. She sees the worried look on my face and says, "Oh don't worry, there ain't nothing up there to hurt anyway."

When she was 107, there developed an irregular heartbeat, and she had to have a pacemaker. At her next birthday party, she is telling us about it – she said, "I asked the doctor how long these things last, and told him I don't want to live forever you know."

From Mom:
We took Grandma out for breakfast. It was a warm day so it was not her birthday. I think that all five boys ordered pancakes and so when the waitress came with the breakfast there were a lot of pancakes. Holding the tray with all those plates as she delivered each meal, she lost it. The tray dumps and a whole pitcher of pancake syrup lands upside down on Grandma's head. Syrup dripped from her hair, her glasses and even her lap.

Restaurant employees arrived to help, but napkins and towels were of no help so we headed to the restroom to do the best we could to clean her up. I was sitting right next to her – why couldn't it have been me. Grandma was calm throughout and never even complained. Another breakfast was provided along with certificates for a hairdresser and dry cleaners. Of course Leo wanted to get a picture outside when we took her back home, but bees started to show up so we had to head inside.

On another trip we took Grandma out to dinner at the Hop Off Inn in Silverton. Back when we were dating, Leo and I often went there to split a B.L.T. and lemonade. We were leaving the restaurant when Grandma looked at a man who was arriving and said "I know you. You sell cars on TV." This from a woman whose sight and hearing were not all that great. Then she launches into his whole routine, complete with gestures and tone of voice. By the end she had an audience who laughed, clapped and cheered. He very graciously, laughed and then bent down and kissed her hand.

On occasion she would tell us that people would ask her what was the secret to her longevity and she said, "I tell them I don't drink and I don't smoke." I think that it also had a lot to do with her walking everywhere. She walked to church every day, to the grocery store and most everywhere she needed to go. Many days she played cards with the other ladies at church.

It was a surprise to me to find out that Great Grandma never owned a home. Turns out she rented the home that I thought she had owned for those many years. Well past 100, the home became too much for her to care for on her own so she moved to an apartment. My brother Jeff lives in the Cincinnati area and helped her move and then helped her move again when the first apartment did not work out well. Each was a second-floor walk-up, which seems it was what she could afford that was still within walking distance of Church and the grocer.

Social Security was enacted in the year 1935, which did not allow enough years of earned income credited for them to be eligible for Social Security. In 1974 the Supplemental Security Income (SSI) program was enacted to help provide for retirees in this gap. At that time, she was 94 and had always managed with little money, but SSI benefits were very low, so Mom and Dad and other family members helped to support her.

SSI benefits were based on income level, and of course Great Grandma claimed the family support as income, which in turn reduced her SSI benefit. There was no point in trying to convince her to not claim the income - there were no gray areas for Great Grandma – you were honest in all things always, regardless the situation, and, you did what was right always, regardless the consequences. May our Lord bless her for having lived it and left the example.

1989 - 110th birthday

At one of her birthday parties she had a cold or the flu. I think it was her 110th. She recalled how it had been easier for her to deal with illness when she was a bit younger. She said, "I want to be with my God." I rarely prayed in those days, but I did ask God to take her to heaven as she had asked. A couple of years later I regretted asking that as I saw my mother grieving at her funeral. I had said, "Mom, she is in a better place now, and she has been wanting to go for some time." Mom knew all of that, but it does not change how much we miss those that have gone on before us.

Here is the rest of the story of that day from Mom:

I knew Grandma was in a better place. My grieving that day had to do with the rosary Leo and I had bought in Rome and given to Grandma. It had been blessed by the

Pope and Grandma treasured it. Grandma thought it had been stolen when she was living in the nursing home. (She moved into the nursing home at 107 after her surgery for the pacemaker.) Turns out that Sue or Bert had taken it home for safekeeping since some of her costume jewelry had gone missing in the nursing home.

Bert and Sue made sure the rosary was placed in Grandma's hands at her funeral, and had arranged for it to be given to me after the funeral. Suddenly I could not bear that happening. I could not take the rosary from her. I found Leo and asked him to go with me to stop that from happening. She had so little in life I could not take it from her.

I pray a lot more these days; usually a few times a day. Before starting the rosary on the way home from work, I ask Great Grandma and other relatives in heaven to pray with me as I pray for them and all of you. I know that it is with their help that so many prayers are answered. Her name is Nettie Huber if you would like to ask her to pray with you as well.

Great Grandma – age 100

173

Pick Me - March 20, 2015

At St. Patrick's we have a Children's Liturgy during Mass at 5 p.m. and 10 a.m. It gives the kids an opportunity to hear and engage in the scripture and gospel readings at a depth oriented to their age. They go to the chapel before the first reading and return to their family during the offertory hymn.

Marilyn and I have been doing the Children's Liturgy for about a year now and really enjoy it. The kids are very engaged and eagerly volunteer for the reading parts. Diane sends resource materials to the volunteer leaders to help us present age-appropriate. I also read the reflections in the Laudate app to help with my understanding.

The Scripture and Gospel readings are interactive – I ask them questions about what they heard and how it fits their lives. There is almost never a shortage of hands wanting to answer the questions or offer their thoughts.

Sunday, March 1st the reading is Romans 8:31, 38-39. Paul's letter to the Romans is explaining God's love for us - it starts out - "Brothers and Sisters: What can we say about all this? If God is on our side, can anyone be against us?" The resource materials suggest asking the kids if they play games that have sides, such as soccer, baseball, basketball, etc.

Of course most have and then the suggestion is to ask what they think Paul means when he says "God is on our side." Their answers are many and perceptive. These are mostly grades three through six with an occasional seventh and eighth grader. Their answers can cause you to sometimes forget how young they are.

Dominic is in seventh grade and so only goes to the Children's Liturgy with Marilyn and me. He helps with setup and helps find someone to carry the candle. He feels he should let someone else do it as he is too old now.

Walking out of church, after Mass, Dominic says, "Dad, you did a good job today." I say, "Thank you, I'm glad you enjoyed it." Then I ask, "So, sometimes I do better than others?" He pauses and answers, "Some days you really nail it," and leaves it at that. How my twelve-year-old son has learned to be so gracious, I don't understand. I certainly was not at that age and struggle even today.

Dominic goes on, "That part about the picking sides for a team was really good." I tell him it came from the materials that Mrs. Miller sends. Dominic says, "And you used it." I ask him if he liked the part about Abraham Lincoln, "I know that God is on our side, but it is my constant and fervent prayer that this nation and I are on God's side."

He didn't answer right away and so I'm guessing it didn't hit home. It is one of my favorite quotes and so had added it to illustrate how important it is for us to be on God's side. Perhaps it is better suited for when they are older. That occurred to me when adding it to my notes during preparation, but had hoped that for some it may linger in their thoughts.

Thinking of our Lord as a team captain picking people for his team I imagine myself like Donkey at the beginning of the Shrek DVD running around behind the crowd, jumping high to be seen, saying, "Pick me! Pick me!"

Abraham Lincoln is remembered as one of our greatest presidents. He brought us through one of the darkest times in our history and set us on a new path - each day asking the grace of wisdom and leadership, knowing he could not get there on his own.

What a different world this would be if each nation's leader did the same "a constant and fervent prayer that they and their nation are on God's side." How much better our country could be if all of our leaders did the same.

It is not possible to know the heart of every person for which we vote. Though none are perfect, for many it is clear they are on our Lord's team. I believe it should be our compass for which we choose.

In Matthew 7:16, Jesus explains how we can know who is on his team. It begins, "You will know them by their fruits. Are grapes gathered from thorns, or figs from thistles?"

May the Lord Bless and Keep you.

A Poem for Mom's 85th birthday - March 21, 2015

Mom and Dad came up to spend the weekend with all of us to celebrate Mom's 85th birthday. Dad had arranged a dinner for Saturday night. My brothers and I debated what to do for Mom. In past years the five of us had done our famous Blues Brothers routine for Mom's 70th and 80th birthdays and Mom and Dad's 50th wedding anniversary.

It is a bit of a roast of Mom and Dad and us. We had changed it up each time, and every time there were a lot of laughs especially from Mom and Dad.

Steve suggested doing a poem and so the search began to find a poem, preferably with five stanzas, one for each of us to recite. Dan Fogleberg's song, *The Leader of the Band*, came to mind and so began the process to borrow the lyrics and make them our own. Wendy also helped with wording.

Below is the poem written and performed in honor of Mom's 85th birthday.

A pretty woman and a handsome man
In the year of 52 were wed
To them five boys were born
Eleven years the spread

They built a life full of life
Many joys and many pains

178

If they had to do it over again
They would do it just the same

We tell our children stories
Of growing up with Mom and Dad
And they will tell their children
Of the example showed to us
It gives us all direction
And foundations made of stone

The leaders of the band are here
And their eyes are growing old
But their blood runs through our hearts
And their words are in our souls
We are just a living legacy
To the leaders of the band

We thank you for the teaching
All the lessons we still hold
We thank you for the freedom
When it came each our time to go
We thank you for the kindness
And the times when you got tough
And, Mom and Dad we don't think we said
"I love you" near enough

The Cup Has Been Taken - May 22, 2015

We had some good news last week; turns out Dominic will not have heart surgery this summer. A little over two weeks ago we went for another round of tests. It was the usual echocardiogram, electrocardiogram, and other tools used to track his heart.

Dr. Russell, his cardiologist, comes in to chat afterward. Last fall when they did the testing they found his right ventricle had enlarged and there was no doubt he needed surgery come summer. This time he is not as certain and is going to meet with the other cardiologists and surgeons the following week.

After discussion there is a vote and it was unanimous for no surgery this year. It seems the deciding factor was that Dominic has no symptoms - he is a full-speed-ahead kid that plays hard all day. He will need to have it done eventually, but it could be a year or two or more. Age 18 or 19 is the longest they will let him go. This team at U of M is as good as there is and we will go with what they recommend. It is never an exact science, but they know how to balance the risks.

Putting a valve in via catheter is available now but must attach to the existing valve. Dominic's heart repair at birth involved losing the valve for the pulmonary artery and so is not a candidate for the catheter. Plus, at 12 years old his vessels are not large enough for the catheter. Each year brings better technologies, and so each year improves the chances of putting the valve in via catheter rather than open heart surgery.

Asking Dominic what he said when he found out, he said, "I shouted at the top of my lungs, woo-hoo! I don't have to have heart surgery this summer." I didn't do any shouting but said thank you to our Lord again and again.

Thank you to all of you praying with us. A week ago Wednesday, when we were coming home from baseball practice, Dominic said, "Dad, your prayers were answered, and everyone praying with us..." "Yes they were," I agreed and we talked again about the people praying with us; the many replies to the note and the many we talked with. Thank you. Thank you. Thank you.

Later that night, before we began our evening prayer, Dominic said, "The cup has been taken from me." "Yes it has," I agreed.

This is the prayer we added to our evening prayer last fall - "Lord, if it is your will, let this cup be taken from this boy so he may not have open heart surgery." We said it every evening we were together.

When we first started saying the prayer, Dominic had asked, "What does it mean to take this cup?" I asked, "Do you remember when Jesus went to pray in the Garden after the Last Supper, it was just before the soldiers took him?" He said, "Yes." I told him how Jesus prayed to the Father asking if it is his will, this cup be taken from him. Jesus' cup was the scourging and crucifixion.

"Your cup is the heart surgery, and I borrowed the prayer from Jesus." As he was falling off to sleep, Dominic said, "Prayers are shared; not borrowed." "Yes they are," I agreed, and now the cup has been taken.

May the Lord bless and keep you, may He let his face shine upon you, and give you his peace.

Two is Not None - June 6, 2015

Mom and Dad spend their winter on Seabrook Island, South Carolina. My brothers and I all try to get there around Easter most years. We would all descend at once back when everyone had kids in school. Mom and Dad would rent another house to fit everyone. Now most of the kids are grown and schedules are more flexible.

Winter break is now the first week of April which sometimes falls on Easter. Most recent years we had been there with Greg and Wendy which worked great for Dominic as he enjoyed hanging out with his cousins Chase and Jason.

This year Katie and Ryan were able to come with Grace, one, and Kamren, four. I think it was the first time being there with Katie and Ryan since they had gotten engaged there seven years ago. It was my first time there with grandchildren. Always the youngest on both sides of the family, now Uncle Dominic is the big kid helping to watch out for the little ones. Of course he loves playing with them as well.

Seabrook is a great place to spend time with family. There are a lot of fun things to do and you can be very busy and very relaxed at the same time. In front of their house is a tidal creek where sometimes dolphins swim by and everyone goes out to watch. Dolphin watching is a favorite pastime and Kamren and Grace got their first taste when Mom and Dad took them all out in the boat.

One morning there were several sitting around the kitchen table talking about dolphins and that they had not come by the house. I had seen one earlier that day and Marilyn had seen one the day before. Kamren is busy looking at something on the table.

We mention the dolphins we saw and he says without looking up, "Two is not none." Laughing, I agree, "Two is not none." We never tire of watching for them no matter how many times we see them and always look forward to seeing them again.

Seems that is true of many things in our lives. We never tire of doing some of our favorite things and never tire of spending time with family and friends – always looking forward to seeing them again.

I have wondered if that is true for our Lord. Does he tire of watching us? I don't think so. We are his children and he enjoys our company, no matter it is one of our good days or not so good. This has become clear from being a parent and a grandparent. We love them and cherish them, and enjoy their company, on their good days and their not so good. Perhaps this is as close as there is to understanding God's love for us.

I find myself spending more time with our Lord in the last many years. Perhaps it just comes with getting older, but there is so much to be grateful. Each day begins thanking him for a good night's sleep. In years past the troubles of the day invaded the time for sleep. Peace is his gift to us, but there was none until coming to know him, spending time with him. Experiencing Christ's peace is understanding he only expects our best every day and trusting him for everything else, including forgiveness of our failings.

The readings at Mass in the days after Easter Sunday are of the time our risen Lord Jesus spent with his disciples before his ascension into Heaven. There is much to teach for them to go and build the church. John 14:27 is well known as we hear part of it on Sunday. "I leave you peace. My peace I give you; not as the world gives do I give to you. Do not let your heart be troubled, nor let it be fearful."

Still there are times most days we need to be drawn back to him, reminding us to trust him and thank him. It is easy to take for granted the blessings in our lives – perhaps thinking it was our own doing, or it was earned, or attributing to luck. Knowing we can do nothing without him gives us the courage to trust in the abilities he has given and the grace that will come for the task and the day.

It is also easy to not be satisfied with the blessings received when forgetting from where they come. Seeing each as a gift from our Lord is to rejoice in our dependence on him and his love for us – to see as a child sees a gift from their parents, their face shining as they run to hug them. And when I forget, I will try to remember that two is not none.

God Bless.

Grieve Loudly - July 24, 2015

Sunday, June 28th I arrive early for church to set up for Children's Liturgy, stopping in the pew for a moment to ask the Lord for help presenting his words. Ben walks in as I am getting up and we shake hands and say hello. Ben asks, "How are you doing?" After a pause, the answer is, "I grieve for my country." Ben looks at me and says, "Grieve loudly." "I will," is my answer.

Two days prior our Supreme Court legalized gay marriage in a decision without basis in our Constitution, much less our history. For many days after there was heaviness in my heart. Never having been good at putting labels on feelings, it took until Sunday morning to realize I was grieving.

Some of the consequences to come we already know well. Many florists, photographers and bakers have been bullied, unjustly fined and put out of business for refusing to participate in a gay wedding. They risk losing everything but still stand for their belief that marriage is between one man and one woman – may God bless them for their courage. Many of their stories can be found at http://www.freetobelieve.com/

Laws requiring equal adoption access for gay couples have forced some Catholic Charities to close their adoption and foster care programs – Boston in 2006, Washington DC in 2010 and Illinois in 2011, as well as England in 2010. Two of my grandchildren came through Catholic Charities –the adoption was final over a year ago for one, and the other is in process.

Adoption and foster care are core functions of Catholic Charities and the tragedy of losing them lives in the faces of the many children in need. These are terrible choices forced upon them. Yet they cannot step away from Church teaching and so I pray for our Bishops; the weight must be difficult to bear.

Our Lord was clear on the subject many times in the old and the new words he gave us. Perhaps it was because he knew how easily we set aside something only mentioned once or twice. Even for those who do not believe, there is an evident natural order to all of creation that can no more be denied than fully understood.

It is our arrogance or perhaps ignorance to think it is we who can define how it is to be. Did we create the heavens and the earth? Did we have anything to do with bringing the creatures or the trees and plants to be here? What about the mountains, plains and waters? How about the rhythm that both sustains life and continually makes it new again – did we do that? He is God and we are not. He created marriage, we did not.

For our support of natural marriage, we are labeled extremists and gay haters when the opposite is true. The Catholic Church is the most welcoming place on earth. Of course gay marriage and gay relationships are not condoned any more than an unmarried man and woman living together. Jesus welcomed sinners so to bring them healing and the way to a better life. So it is with the Church. It is why we are all here – none are saints – we need his forgiveness and healing and grace – the way to a better life.

Having been divorced twice, I have no credibility when it comes to speaking on marriage. Yet I believe in it and the purpose for which God created it – it is our foundation from which we build our world.

So what is next? One clue comes from testimony in the case. Obergefell v. Hodges was the combination of four cases against states with laws banning gay marriage. Shamefully, Donald Verrilli, the US Solicitor General, was one of the attorneys for the plaintiffs. His job is to represent the interests of the United States government in cases before the Supreme Court. Why is it that the interests of the United States government are in opposition to the laws of our states – 31 states had constitutional amendments banning gay marriage and almost all the rest had various laws banning gay marriage.

During the case Justice Samuel Alito asked Verrilli, "In the Bob Jones case, the Court held that a college was not entitled to tax-exempt status if it opposed interracial marriage or interracial dating. So would the same apply to a university or a college if it opposed same-sex marriage?" Verrilli answered, "It's certainly going to be an issue. I don't deny that."

So, we know that the tax-exempt status will be in question for any organization that supports natural marriage, including all churches. Already there have been many calling for the government to revoke their tax-exempt status and recent history has proven the administration, and some in the IRS, have no problem improperly using their position to silence religious and conservative voices.

We know that prosecutions will continue for any business refusing to participate in a gay wedding. Now it will extend to churches. We know prosecutions and lawsuits will accelerate now for any adoption and foster care organization declining to place a child with a gay couple. Most will probably close their doors.

Hundreds of county clerks have refused to issue marriage licenses to gay couples. Some have resigned while others stand as a lightning rod. A judge in Ohio refused to officiate a gay wedding. All of these because they believe marriage is between one man and one woman – no court can force them to do otherwise. May God bless them for their courage.

Many states have passed, or are working on laws such as the Religious Freedom Restoration Act which protect people and their organizations from prosecution for taking a stand on natural marriage. Congress is also working on such a bill. It is perhaps our only chance to keep our religious freedom.

Even if we are able to pass such laws to protect our religious freedom, there are many that will continue vilifying the Church. Those strong in their faith will stand with the Church, but some may use this as the reason to distance themselves. Some will use this to draw others away from the Church. They will need our prayers as the Lord spoke many times about those that would lead us on the wrong path:

Jeremiah 23:1 "Woe to the shepherds who mislead and scatter the flock of my pasture, says the Lord."

Isaiah 5:20 "Woe to those who call evil good and good evil, who put darkness for light and light for darkness, who put bitter for sweet and sweet for bitter!"

Matthew 18:5-6 "Whoever receives one such child in my name receives me; but whoever causes one of these little ones who believe in me to sin, it would be better for him to have a great millstone fastened round his neck and to be drowned in the depth of the sea."

This last one is repeated in Mark 9:42 and Luke 17:2. Jesus is speaking of children and adults – he uses the term "Little Ones" for his disciples in Matthew 10:42.

For those who stand with the Church, Jesus said many times to his disciples, "Be not afraid." And so it is we are called to have courage in this difficult time – everything has changed and yet nothing has changed.

May the Lord bless and keep you, may He let his face shine upon you, and be gracious to you, and give you his peace.

Bindings - August 31, 2015

Last month Katie and son-in-law Ryan had come with Grace, (one and a half) and Kamren, (four and a half), to spend some time on the lake and son Ryan came with Bastian (one and a half). We were on the lake from early morning until evening.

Grace and Bastian always pair up quickly, and Bastian is happy to have Grace lead the way on their adventures. Kamren loves hanging with Uncle Dominic and Dominic is very good with all the grandkids. It was a perfect day weather-wise, and we had a great time as they all love playing in the water.

After dinner they pack up to head home. I'm tucking Grace in her car seat and struggling with the straps and buckles. Kamren is in the far back ready to go. He says, "Goodbye Grandpa," but I'm concentrating on the buckles and give no response. Finishing, I give Grace a kiss and close her door. As the door is shutting Kamren says again, "Goodbye Grandpa," this time in earnest.

Walking around the back of the car and stepping in the other side, Kamren's face lights up. Crawling back to him, we give tight hugs before saying goodbye.

Thoughts of those moments flowed through many times in the days after, making it clear there would be a note going out. As usual there is only the seed, not knowing the story to be told. Each time it only requires to begin and the seed becomes the story. For a time, the "Grieve Loudly" note delayed this writing, and then gently I am reminded to begin.

It feels like a great honor for it to have been so important for grandpa to say goodbye – the look of concern on his face instantly turning to a big smile the moment my head peeked through the door.

Moments such as this forever bind our hearts to each in our family. Or is it how our Lord made us - binding us to one another - that create these wonderful moments dotting our lives? Perhaps it is both.

How many times have one of mine been left with a look of concern on their face, when simply being aware I could have turned it into a smile? Too many is certain. But the forgiveness and understanding that is family gives us every day the opportunity to start anew.

A month prior, Mom and Dad invited all of us to meet for dinner in Chelsea to celebrate their 63rd anniversary. Not all could make it, but quite a few were there. During dinner Mom and Dad talked a bit about the family – how they are grateful how everyone gets along so well – how every family gathering is a joy to watch and remember - and how it is not so with all families.

Five years ago Mom and Dad had sent a note out to the five sons on this topic asking our thoughts. Responses covered a lot of ground but much pointed to our relationship with God and the example given by Mom and Dad.

Our family is far from perfect and we have had our share of disagreements and skirmishes and probably will again. Forgiveness and understanding always seem to win out somehow.

Greg mentioned, "We're too thick-skinned to let a rift boil into something major and too thick-headed to know when our feelings should be hurt." I certainly fit the thick-headed part.

Jeff's thoughts included, "When there is an issue today you can see how people not in the conflict give space and the most important thing they do is not choose sides. This comes from a built up respect for each other and realizing this is a bump in the road."

As told in the book of Genesis, chapter 17, God made a covenant with Abraham to bless him and his descendants and make them a blessing to all nations. Their part to keep the covenant was to have him as their God and no other. God renewed this covenant many times through the ages with Abraham's descendants. Finally, Jesus came to make the covenant with all of us.

Of the blessings he has given during our time on earth, I think the greatest is a family to love. And so his plan seems clear – when we are a blessing to our family we are a blessing to all the lives we touch and all the lives they touch...

The Stowaway - October 1, 2015

Labor Day weekend we spent at my parents' house in Indiana. Not all can make it every year but it is always a large group – 37 including eight great-grandchildren this year. The weather was great and it was a lot of fun for everyone, as always. Having my three grandchildren there was especially fun.

Everyone is tired after making the drive home Monday afternoon. I take Dominic back to his Mom's and then ask Marilyn if she would like to go for a pontoon ride. Turns out the battery is dead so instead we head out on the ski boat.

We are just into the bay with the public boat launch when we are startled by a raccoon suddenly appearing in the bow of the boat. He slowly walks around on the seats and then looks over the edge hoping for an escape. Seeing the water, he decides to hide under the rail but it is a small space and so is still visible.

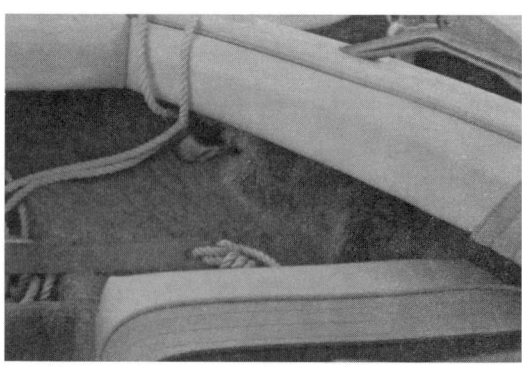

Not wanting to make the trip all the way back home with our passenger, I suggest we beach the boat at the launch to see if he will hop out. There is one boat pulling out and another waiting to launch as we beach. I tell them of our situation and they all hop in their boats. Perhaps to wait and see if I can persuade the raccoon to move on, or, to avoid the potential of an ornery critter coming near. Marilyn goes out the back of the boat and waits in the water.

Waiting for a bit to see if he will realize we have stopped moving, he doesn't budge. Then getting the boat hook, I try prodding him a bit but it seems no amount of encouragement is going to get him to move. He only tucks himself tighter under the rail.

We decide to risk heading back home and of course about half way there he comes out and again takes a look over the edge. Seeing the water again he goes back to his "hiding spot." Once parked, I pull the stern of the boat close to the side of the boat lift, giving him an exit path.

Then we sit on the deck and watch for a bit.

Awhile later he is walking around in the boat but sees us and ducks down again. Finally, he gets out, walks up the dock, then the yard and heads under the deck. Seems we are not to be rid of him anytime soon.

Later that evening I called Dominic about something else and told him the story of our little adventure. He thought it was hilarious and told me to tell Marilyn he was proud of her for not freaking out.

As we sometimes do, this poor raccoon just picked the wrong boat. When presented with an exit he was too afraid to take a look. No amount of prodding would get him to even consider the opportunity at hand, clinging ever tighter to his crevice. Twice he tried to find his own path but only found deep water a long distance from shore.

Again a new path is offered, and still, he clings to a hopeless position, too afraid to even peek out. After some quiet time, he gathers his courage to sneak around a bit to see where he is. Taking a chance, he steps out and chooses the way to freedom.

Hindsight can be a great teacher – seeing how much life is really about the choices we make. So many times taking my own road rather than one offered by our Lord and then too long clinging to a hopeless direction. Always there is the way back regardless the number of bad choices.

It is in quiet time, in conversation with him, that we find what he wants for us and the courage to step out. He puts people in our lives to help us. Parents he instills with the endless yearning to help their children choose well.

In turn, he puts people in our lives, in need of our help. It is where we find our own capacity. And it is where we come to know the peace and joy in helping others on their journey.

May the boat you choose be always from the Lord.

Monsters - November 7, 2015

One lesson learned from my parents is when you don't have something nice to say about someone, say nothing at all. I don't remember them saying the words but I do remember the example.

Still it seems, we are occasionally compelled to call it as we see it. Ronald Reagan labeled Soviet Russia the "Evil Empire" in 1983. This was after he had witnessed John Paul II teaching of the dignity of every person and the injustice of restricting religious freedom – this directed at the Soviet rule of his native Poland.

Visiting Poland in 1979 teaching this message, the people responded by chanting, "We want God, we want God, we want God in the family, we want God in the schools, we want God in our books."

Though disputed by some, the credible story is Soviet leadership then directed the KGB to use all possible means to end the threat created by the new Pope, "…if necessary beyond disinformation and discrediting." In 1981 John Paul II was shot by an assassin hired by the Bulgarian secret police, ordered by the KGB. His survival seemed quite miraculous and his grace and dignity made him much loved and admired around the world.

Some historians credit the words from John Paul II and Ronald Reagan with the fall of the Berlin Wall in 1989 and the dissolution of the Soviet Union two years later. Such words, consistently delivered, resonate in the minds of the people watching from the outside and the inside, changing the path of history.

Jesus also used tough words, referring several times to the "evil generation," making clear there is a path to life and a path to destruction.

In our country, in this day, there is a group of people and companies in the business of killing human babies and selling their organs and body parts. The horror of this has been exposed to the world by The Center for Medical Progress (CMP).

Beginning in July this year they released a series of undercover videos revealing a story that probably none would believe without the video evidence. Spending a couple hours on their website, http://www.centerformedicalprogress.org/, left me drained and troubled. The realities detailed there are so unsettling I don't recommend anyone visit. Following are some of the things that struck me.

Selling baby body parts is illegal, and yet there are a number of companies in the business of harvesting them at abortion clinics and selling them to research labs. One company, StemExpress, has nearly 100 abortion clinics they work with and about half are Planned Parenthood clinics (PP).

PP does pre-screening on the women who are potential abortion clients and sends the information to companies like StemExpress. They compare the information with the orders they have for organ and body parts, so they know where and when to send their harvest teams.

PP would ask the expectant mother to sign a form prior to the abortion, consenting to "donation" of the aborted baby to research. Everything on the form expressed in terms to hide the reality of what would happen.

PP could not have the harvest team show up with no babies to dissect so they would tell the woman they could not do the abortion if she did not sign the consent form. Later PP executives decided the mother's signature was not necessary as it was probably not legally required and there was no way the mother could know what happened to her baby.

Larger babies are more valued due to larger and more fully developed organs, but traditional methods left nothing useable. So they change the abortion procedure to get more intact babies – procedures that are incredibly painful to the baby and more dangerous to the mother. Some use the illegal partial-birth abortion method and on occasion babies are born alive - still they harvest the parts.

StemExpress, and the other organ brokers, pay the abortion clinic for each organ and body part harvested and then sells them to the highest bidder. Demand is high and profits are large.

It leaves you wondering how any of them could ever get their mind to accept that any of this was anything but evil. Perhaps years in the abortion business, trying to justify it to themselves and others, has subdued any sense of right and wrong. And so it is they have become monsters.

Many in the abortion industry have left - some because of those praying outside their clinics - and some have become strong pro-life supporters. So we continue to pray for them and the mothers and babies.

Two and a half years ago the story of Kermit Gosnell unfolded and was almost entirely ignored by the media. PP was mute on the topic, probably because they knew many of their clinics were no better. The note that I wrote about it is "Born and Unborn" on the website www.wordsfrommyfather.com on the 2013 page.

Fortunately, these videos from CMP could not entirely be ignored by our liberal media, and was enough to bring a congressional investigation. So far no criminal charges have been brought but Texas has raided three clinics, and we hope other states will do so as well. Already several states have ended funding to PP.

Several attempts have been launched by the Republicans to eliminate PP's $500 million in federal funding. So far the Democrats have succeeded in blocking every attempt and President Obama has promised to veto any bill that defunds PP.

For every PP clinic there are 20 community health clinics providing all the same services as PP, with the exception of abortion. There are no legitimate arguments to continue funding PP. There is only the money trail from PP to the Democrats.

"Men occasionally stumble over the truth, but most of them pick themselves up and hurry off as if nothing had happened." Sir Winston Churchill.

Perpetuating lies to justify their continued support of PP makes them as guilty as those killing the babies.

Such words, consistently delivered, will resonate in the minds of the people watching from the outside and the inside, thus changing the path we are on - lest we allow more to become monsters in an evil generation.

Kamren is now Cameron - November 26, 2015

Monday, November 9[th,] daughter Katie and son-in-law Ryan finalized their adoption of Kamren and so Kamren became Cameron McComb. Much of the family came to the courthouse and were treated to a touching presentation by the judge.

She explained this is family court and much of their proceedings are divorces, custody battles, and neglect and abuse cases, none of which are pleasant to hear. However, one day a month they get to do adoptions which they truly enjoy. So the judge thanked Katie and Ryan for coming to the courthouse rather than completing it by mail - they are glad to see and talk with the family rather than just signing off on the papers.

She talked about the importance of family support and the presence of so many said all that was needed. In the courtroom were Ryan's parents, Kim and Mary, and brother Jaime; Katie's mom Mary and husband Paul; and daughter Becca and me.

I don't think there was a dry eye in the courthouse as she finished. Ryan took a moment to thank everyone that had helped them in the process. The judge had been with them since they first brought him home as a foster child. Three women from Catholic Charities were there that had placed Cameron with them a little over two years ago and then helped them through the adoption.

Cameron owned a place in my heart from the beginning. He desperately needed a mom and dad, and it was clear how good Katie and Ryan were for him. We never know for certain which way life is going to turn, but God has a way of letting us know how things might go.

On the website www.wordsfrommyfather.com there are some notes that touch on parts of the story of Cameron. On the 2014 page there are four:

- "Two Stories" includes the telling of when Cameron came to Katie and Ryan as a foster child in August of 2013.
- "The Path to Grace Elizabeth" tells the story of adopting Grace with Cameron woven in.
- "The Spirit of Christmas" is about him learning about Christmas.
- "Coming Home" tells about beginning the adoption process a little over a year ago.

Also on the 2015 page, there are two - "Two is not none" and "Bindings."

Becca rode with me on the round trip to attend the adoption. We don't get to see each other too often, and I very much enjoyed our conversations. We spent much of it talking about Grace and Cameron and Bastian. The time we get to spend with our grown children seems to become less all the time. They have busy lives of their own and at family gatherings much of the time is spent with the grandchildren.

The prior weekend my son Ryan had called to see if we wanted to stop by. They had just moved into their new home. We had several events that weekend but stopped over one evening. They were busy painting and so Dominic and Marilyn and I spent the evening playing with grandson Bastian.

Seems it often goes this way with grandchildren and grandparents and we treasure every moment. We get to be a part of our kids becoming parents and our grandkids each becoming their own person.

Many of you had included Cameron and Katie and Ryan in your prayers, bringing them God's grace and peace on this journey. Thank you, thank you, thank you. God does answer prayers, and this time it is a little boy named Cameron. I find myself thanking our Lord again and again.

Happy Thanksgiving and may God bless you and keep you.

Cozy as a Puppy - December 17, 2015

On a Thursday morning, two weeks before Christmas, I had been up early working on a note about our blessed mother, Mary. It had been in the works for more than a week, hoping to have it out by Christmas.

While in the shower it becomes clear this one will be awhile before it is sent out. We are in the middle of a bible study on Mary and have about two months remaining. To try to finish it now will be to miss the depth that comes with each session. My understanding grows more from our group discussions than any amount of reading on my own.

Still in the shower, I'm hoping there will be a note or two to write before completing the one about Mary. And yet each tends to be all consuming and so it seems unlikely there can be two in process. Perhaps the Mary note can be put away for a time and then get it back out.

Getting dressed for work after the shower, I go and wake up Dominic. As is our routine, we sit in the La-Z-Boy for a bit while he wakes up and give him his blessing. We look out at the lake but the morning has not shown first light, and so all is dark outlines with the faint light from homes.

Dominic curls up tightly and says, "I'm as cozy as a puppy." "Me too," I say. As he is 13, there may not be too much longer he will want to sit in my lap to start our mornings, and we talk a little about that. For now, there is no better way to start the day.

I tell Dominic, "When you are grown you will find you can still feel cozy as a puppy. It will come with knowing God is always with you, getting to know him and trusting him." Though unsaid, it somehow seems Dominic wonders if it can be the same feeling, but I know it will and ever more enduring.

Some minutes later, facing the microwave while making our oatmeal, it becomes clear our Lord had just given a note to write, answering the silent prayer. Tears of gratitude drip down my face but quickly wipe them away so Dominic doesn't wonder why his dad is crying over oatmeal. Being 13 he already is growing in the opinion that his dad is a bit daft at times.

Merry Christmas and may you feel as cozy as a puppy this Christmas and every day.

There are no Words - December 31, 2015

In the early part of October, Dominic had a trip to the emergency room for what turned out to be an inguinal hernia. Something I had not heard of, but a fairly common occurrence for boys we are told. After getting things back in their right places, the ER doctors told us we needed to schedule a surgical repair at a pediatric hospital to prevent recurrences.

We met with a team at the U of M Mott Children's Hospital and scheduled the surgery for mid-November. Dominic had a productive cough on the day of surgery and so we were sent home as it was not worth the risk of intubation. It was rescheduled, and we returned December 16th for surgery.

They are very good at taking care of both the patient and the family gathered. My respect for the medical profession grows with every experience, seeing their professionalism and focus and caring. This is only reinforced by three nieces in the medical profession; hearing them talk about their jobs and patient situations.

In pre-op, the anesthesiologist comes in to talk with us. She tells Dominic that 13 is the age they switch from the mask to the IV and asks if he thinks he will be okay with that. Dominic tells her, "I will be freaking out on the inside but I will be fine on the outside." True to his word he barely winces when the needle goes in but gets very pale and lightheaded before they are finished.

There are all manners of entertainment to keep kids occupied in pre-op. Dominic's mother Patti, her mother Gina, and her sister Leah talk and text other family members while Dominic and I play on the Xbox. Surgery was scheduled for 1:00 but it is about 20 minutes after 2:00 before they take Dominic.

Patti, Gina, and I head to the cafeteria as no one has eaten since breakfast. It is expected to be a two-hour surgery, and they have given us a restaurant-style pager for updates on the process. Grabbing a sandwich and a banana I sit down at a table and wait for them.

All of the compartmentalized fear and anxiety washes over me and so bow my head and ask our Lord to watch over Dominic and to guide the hands of the doctors and nurses. I finish by giving thanks for my meal and the tsunami is gone.

A few minutes later, Patti has set her food down and is busy gathering utensils and stuff. She is having difficulty keeping her composure and begins to come apart as she sits down. I tell her, "Say a prayer." Repeating, "Just bow your head and say a prayer." She bows her head and a moment later looks up and says, "I have no words." But the words are not important as God knows our needs and her composure has returned.

It is a couple minutes before 3:00 when the pager goes off telling us the surgeon is ready to meet. This causes some unspoken concern since it has only been about 40 minutes. We head up to what is known as the "Frog" desk. There is a large metal sculpture of a frog on the wall behind the reception desk. They put us in a consultation room and the surgeon comes in with an odd expression on his face.

He greets all of us in the room and begins, "So here is the thing. I made the incision and followed the tubes to where the hernia should be and there was no hernia. We moved the dressings to find the mark made in pre-op to make sure we were on the correct side. Then went back and checked the original paperwork to check again that we had the correct side. I even had everyone in the room come and look to confirm they saw what I was seeing. I did put a couple of stitches to reinforce the area where the hernia should have been."

He pauses a moment, looks at us and says, "I never saw one heal itself before." Then asks, "You guys know there was a hernia right?" I answer, "Yes, we were in the emergency room with him at Huron Valley Hospital when they found the hernia." Then go on to tell about Dominic throwing up three times on the way there from the pain; about watching the doctor and ultrasound tech find the path taken by his intestines through the inguinal canal. And watching as two ER doctors worked to Massage the intestines back into place.

The surgeon looked a bit relieved. I tell him, "We had a similar experience last May when Dominic was to have a pulmonary valve put in. A year ago they found his right ventricle was enlarged and so it was important to put in the valve before there was any damage to his heart. When May came, they ran the same tests again and the decision is we don't need to do it now."

A note titled "The Cup Has Been Taken" tells the story of getting a pass on imminent heart surgery. It is on the website www.wordsfrommyfather.com dated May 2015.

Sometimes when our Lord touches our lives it is more apparent than others. This fills my thoughts as we say our thanks to the surgeon and head back to the waiting room until Dominic is allowed visitors. So many prayers for Dominic from so many people and there are no words to express the gratitude in my heart.

Relating the story many times, most recognize it as the Lord's work. Saturday before Christmas our Boy Scout troop is gathered at St. Pat's to distribute ham orders. One of the scout moms tells a similar story with her two boys. She says, "Prayer is a powerful thing. I could tell you many more." But they have hams to deliver and are on their way.

Talking with mom and dad the next day, they ask if Dominic is feeling like he had an unnecessary surgery, or is happy he won't have the many weeks of recovery. He seems to waver between the two even when I point out the only way the doctors could know it had repaired itself was to go in and look.

After we talk about it a couple more times, it becomes apparent he feels there would be no added recovery time had the repair been required - to him the incision is the surgery and he knows how quickly he heals. Plus he is a positive kid spending little time on what might have been.

So it has been many times in my life not seeing the gifts given - perhaps hidden from understanding, or just taken for granted, or believing it was accomplished on my own. Sometimes reminded later, we see more clearly when our perspective has changed a bit. Looking at life with prayer is to see and trust the Lord's hand in our lives and be filled with thanksgiving beyond words.

May the Lord bless and keep you, may He let his face shine upon you and give you his peace.

2016

"We have forgotten God. We have forgotten the gracious hand which preserved us in peace, and multiplied and enriched and strengthened us; and we have vainly imagined, in the deceitfulness of our hearts, that all these blessings were produced by some superior wisdom and virtue of our own."

-- *Abraham Lincoln, proclamation of a national day of prayer,* March 30, 1863

My Name is Mary - February 18, 2016

My name is Mary and I would like to tell you about my life. I will begin in Nazareth when I was betrothed to a wonderful man named Joseph. It was an exciting time filled with the anticipation of beginning our life together. Life took a new direction one day with a startling visit from the angel Gabriel. He told me of things that were difficult to understand.

I am to bear the son of God and his name will be Jesus. It was much to take in and I wondered how this could be. From the time I can remember we were taught the scriptures with the prophecies of the one who is to come. My heart could feel their fulfillment in his words, and so I said to Gabriel, "Let it be done to me as you have said."

Gabriel also said my cousin Elizabeth is six months with child. She was thought to be barren and is many years past childbearing time, and so I went to be with her. Elizabeth's greeting was as wondrous as Gabriel's. Gabriel had greeted me, "Hail Mary full of grace, the Lord is with you." Elizabeth said, "Blessed are you among women and blessed is the fruit of your womb."

She told me the baby in her womb leapt for joy at hearing my voice. Filled with the Holy Spirit she knew I bore the son of God, without me having said a word. Such a joyous time sharing the wonder of these events, rejoicing in the Lord as he has shown great favor to his lowly handmaidens.

We could not know then how our son's lives would come together when it was time for Jesus to begin public life. When Elizabeth's son was grown he became known as John the Baptist; the one sent to prepare the way for Jesus.

After returning to Nazareth, Joseph had been saddened at the news I was expecting a child. In those days' marriage vows began a time of betrothal before living together. He told me he had planned to quietly divorce me, but then an angel came to visit him in a dream. Joseph then understood and took me into his home, becoming the adopted father of the son of God.

From Rome came the decree for a census which required we travel to Bethlehem, the city of Joseph's birth. It is a journey of 80 miles and took many days as my pregnancy was near the end. In Bethlehem there was no place for us to stay as so many had arrived before us. A man told Joseph of a place where we could have a roof over our heads.

Jesus was born, and there came shepherds to see the baby, and they bowed down and worshiped him. They told us of angels coming in the night to tell them of the birth of the savior in Bethlehem. Then came three Magi who also bowed down and worshiped him. They gave gifts of gold, frankincense, and myrrh and told us of their journey following the star.

They also told us of King Herod whom they had visited while still searching for us. Herod had asked they come back and tell him when they found the Christ child. In a dream they were told not to return to Herod and so went home a different way.

As prescribed by our law, we took Jesus for circumcision on the eighth day and then to Jerusalem on the 40th day to present Jesus in the temple and myself for ritual purification. Our offering, as allowed, was two turtledoves since we did not have the means for the offering of a lamb.

There was a man named Simeon in the temple who was filled with the Holy Spirit. Upon seeing Jesus, he took him in his arms and declared out loud that here is the Messiah. He also told of sufferings that will come to me and a sword of sorrow that will pierce my heart. All these things I pondered in my heart, unable to know their full meaning, but knowing God is with us watching over us.

Word spread of Simeon's proclamation in the temple and Joseph was told in a dream to take us into hiding in Egypt as Herod was going to search for Jesus to kill him. Herod became angered when he heard of Simeon's proclamation and knew he had been tricked by the Magi. He knew from the Magi this child would be king of the Jews and feared being replaced by him. Unable to know which was Jesus, he ordered his soldiers to kill all boys two years and younger, in and around Bethlehem. These were the first martyrs for Jesus, and we grieved for them and their families.

After Herod's death an angel came to Joseph in a dream telling us to return to Israel. We learned Herod's son now ruled Judea, making it dangerous to return to Bethlehem. Joseph was told in a dream to take us to the district of Galilee to live in the city of Nazareth. Jesus learned the carpenter trade from Joseph, growing in strength and filled with wisdom.

Every year we made the pilgrimage to Jerusalem for Passover. One time, when Jesus was 12, we had started the journey home and Jesus remained in Jerusalem. Our group was large and we presumed him to be with relatives or friends. Not able to find him after a day's journey, we returned to Jerusalem.

We were frightened as any parents would be, but knew God was watching over him. On the third day we found him in the temple sitting and talking among the teachers who were amazed at his wisdom. Asking why he would do such a thing, he replied "How is it you were looking for me? Did you not know I must be in my father's house?" Joseph and I did not understand his words and so held them in our hearts. We returned to Nazareth, and Jesus was obedient as he had always been.

Jesus was 30 and had just gathered his first few disciples when we were all invited to a wedding in Cana. After some time the wine was running out. This would be embarrassing to the wedding couple and so I went to talk with Jesus, knowing he could help; not knowing how. Jesus answered in a manner leaving me unsure of the meaning and yet I knew he was going to help them. So I said to the servants, "Do whatever he tells you." Jesus had them fill six stone jars with water, each holding 20 to 30 gallons. Then he had them draw from one of the jars and take it to the man in charge of the wedding. It is then we learned the water had been turned to wine.

With this first miracle began Jesus' public life and the fulfillment of his mission. His followers gathered quickly as he taught with the authority of his father and performed many signs over the next few years. Each sign revealed the glory of God and his overflowing generosity, beginning with the first when he gave more than 120 gallons of the finest wine; far more than was needed. When he cured, he also forgave their sins; healing body and soul; healing their hearts.

When his public life was nearing its end, he told his apostles he would be tortured and killed and then raised on the third day. He also told them they would desert him when he was taken. These thoughts were impossible for them to understand; they had given their lives to him and could no more imagine losing him than leaving his side, regardless the consequence.

It came to pass as he said and there we were at Golgotha when they nailed him to the cross. All of the apostles had fled as Jesus told them they would, except John. Grief seemed to want to crush me as I watched with John and the other women. Strength from his words, telling us what would happen, helped sustain us then. And yet knowing who he is, and what is to be, could not diminish the pain of seeing him tortured and killed.

When Jesus saw us standing there by his cross, he said, "Woman behold your son." And to John he said, "Behold your mother." His words went beyond the tender mercy of asking John to provide for me. It was declaring fulfillment of the words to Satan in the Garden of Eden, "I will put enmity between you and the woman, and between your seed and her seed; he shall bruise your head and you shall bruise his heel."

Calling me "woman," as he also had done at the wedding in Cana, proclaimed me as the woman of that passage. It also proclaimed Jesus' sacrifice has crushed Satan's head and his hold on this world. Asking me to be mother to John was him asking me to be mother of all who would be disciples.

After we placed him in the tomb it was a frightening time, just as when we had lost him when he was 12. Knowing he was coming back was a help to us. Jesus came back to us on the third day, rising from the dead as he said. Our grieving became rejoicing and we could feel the joy in heaven flowing through our hearts.

Jesus spent time with his disciples over the next many days, instructing them on building his church. All understood his words with more clarity now. He appeared to many hundreds so it would be witnessed and written by more than his apostles. After a time he ascended into heaven to be with the Father and sent the Holy Spirit to be with us. And so began our mission to build his church and his kingdom here on earth.

I had longed to be in heaven with Jesus but there was work to be done. Mercifully, when it was my time to go, all of the apostles were gathered from distant lands so we could say goodbye. When he took me into heaven, he brought my body as well to make known your temple of the Holy Spirit will also join you here.

And now, my dear children, one of the great pleasures of being mother to all is being asked to pray for you and those in your prayers, and to carry those prayers to my son. There is much joy in heaven as every prayer welcomes the Lord into your life.

Still, Satan roams the earth trying to discourage faith and lead away from the Lord any that he can. Over the centuries I have visited many times around the world to help build the church and strengthen faith, revealing myself to only a few to carry the message. Occasionally Satan has led some to falsely report visits from me, knowing when revealed it will discourage a few from their faith. I come only to bring you to God. From this you can know it is me. But I ask you to remember, as Jesus said, "Blessed are those who have not seen and yet believe."

Jesus came to forgive sins, but denial is often the response to sin, leaving the weight to damage the understanding of right and wrong. Some in time come to deny sin even exists. Thus is denied the need for Jesus and who he is - taking away sin only comes from him. And so the burden of sin remains on so many hearts, perhaps carefully hidden from the mind. Accepting Jesus' forgiveness sets you free, cleansing the darkness from your hearts, making them soft again and open to the grace of the Holy Spirit.

In this Jubilee Year of Mercy, proclaimed by Pope Frances, you are invited to come to know God's mercy and to rejoice in the Lord's forgiveness and the blessings it brings to your life. His mercy is there for all regardless how far away they have been or for how long.

You are also invited to pray and to help spread this message. It can be as simple as sharing inspirational thoughts; perhaps something you have seen or read. An uncomfortable venture for most, and yet the Lord is with you always, watching over you. His words and his grace sustained us in difficult times, and so it is for you. Your heart is aware of all these truths and so now is to believe and be not afraid.

Purpose in life and happiness are the pursuits of all and yet so remote without our Lord. Momentary happiness can be found in many endeavors. Something enduring is only found in Jesus. Bring my son into the lives of your family, and those around you, and you will bring them peace, purpose and happiness. There is no greater gift.

Peace be with you.

Telling the Story - April 6, 2016

In September our Bible study group started a study on our blessed mother, Mary. As it progressed, much was learned, planting the need to share. Writing began around the first of December for the note that became "My Name is Mary." It is on the website www.wordsfrommyfather.com. Little more than a week into writing it became clear this one would take some time - there was two months remaining in the Mary Bible study and much left to learn. So it was put away for a while to allow another note to be written.

Then Dominic went in for surgery in mid-December to have an inguinal hernia repaired. It was quite a surprise when the surgeon came back to tell us there was no hernia. "There are no words" is the note telling the story of this experience. It is on the "2015" page of the website.

Just after the note was sent, Dominic read it while we were having breakfast. As he finished we got into a discussion of our thoughts on why God had healed him. It had occupied a bit of my thoughts as he has had many procedures in his 13 plus years. Last spring he gets a pass on heart surgery and this time his hernia is healed. With the gratitude for his blessings also comes wonder as it required surgery to see it had been healed.